THE WARRIOR WITHIN

A GUIDE TO INNER POWER

Shale Paul

To Jack Cook

You'll find this a bit different
than our usual business reading,
perhaps more fun!

Regards,

Shale Paul

1/8/87

DELTA GROUP PRESS
Golden, Colorado

Book Designed and Illustrated by John Kehe

Library of Congress Catalog Card Number 83-72057

ISBN 0-913787-01-9 (Hardcover)

ISBN 0-913787-02-7 (Paperback)

PRINTED IN THE UNITED STATES OF AMERICA

To Blanche

Without her, this book might never have been written. She had her own special vision and believed in mine. She is a close friend and companion, a warrior in her own right, and incidentally, my mother.

TABLE OF CONTENTS

FOREWORD

Having lived and worked on five continents during and since World War II, I thought I had pretty well exhausted my share of exceptional people. Then, in 1974, along came Shale Paul.

My first impression of Shale was accurate enough as far as it went. I saw before me the typical successful WASP businessman, almost a stereotype of the All-American boy who had it made. His credentials were impeccable: MBA, an enviable business record that included a four-year stint with a leading management consulting firm, a former Marine Corps officer, an instrument-rated commercial pilot, a corporate planning expert, head of his own construction-development firm, a summer home on Cape Cod, a real bottom-liner if ever I saw one. And bottom-liners were not necessarily my favorite people.

My first impression, however, had not gone deep enough, and I began to realize there was much more to Shale Paul. Although not a big man, he was physically impressive, and also I sensed within him an inner strength that both intrigued and briefly disturbed me. Power there, but benificent power. So, as he says in chapter 3, I "reluctantly" agreed to accept him as one of my last individual students. Thank God I did, for he has taught me so much.

Shale Paul is an extraordinary human being. *The Warrior Within* is an extraordinary book. Within these pages is a universal truth that shakes me, even though much of what Shale has learned comes from one part of the world, the Far East, especially Japan, that I have never seen. And this book, Shale's book, could not appear at a better time than now. While the whole world is understandably uneasy and millions are losing hope of ever making sense of their lives, Shale offers a viable alternative to the common wisdom that has so clearly failed most of us. He suggests a different way of thinking about ourselves and our worlds. He tells us the observable truth that we have never seen because we have never really been taught how to think clearly and in the requisite depth about ourselves. He is not leading us into mysticism or exotic philosophy, nor is he attempting to dope us with pop psychology. Patiently, he is guiding us into a clearer understanding of our daily experience and giving us a far more effective means of coping with all aspects of our lives.

At first I thought that Shale's way was not my way. We come from two different worlds. My roots are in the Highlands and the Isle of Skya in both Americas, Europe, Africa, and the Middle East, while Shale has learned immensely from the Orient. Yet it should not have surprised me that basic truths gleaned from the world overflow naturally together. In truth, there is but one way for all of us in the end: harmony, dynamic balance, peace, Shalom, Salaam, Pace. And no one knows it better than that human paradox, the canny, experienced, self-disciplined warrior.

The Warrior Within, therefore, is not a strange choice of title, for the Oriental martial arts so familiar to Shale are not martial in purpose. They are a means to an end. That end is peace, threatening to no one else.

Look around you. The world seems populated by nasty, aggressive people. Yet we all know some gentle giants too, powerful people at peace with the world because they are at peace with themselves. A state to be envied. *The Warrior Within* lights the path toward such powerful peace, for all with the courage to seek it.

I have been called a counselor, a teacher, a mentor. Whatever I am, I have been trying to help others learn to be themselves, in peace, for more than a quarter of a century. In the fifties, my clients were almost invariably white, male, middle-class executives and professionals. Today the classes conducted by our center are made up of as many women as men, representatives of all races, professions, and trades, from ages fifteen to seventy plus. In these times of dislocating flux and radical change, no one knows how many Americans are leading lives of quiet desperation. Millions, however, are anxiously seeking help in an effort to sort things out. They may not know what they're looking for, but they do know that they want something else in their lives, and the growth of their search is obvious. The counseling business is booming, and self-help books and articles pour from the presses in an endless stream. Yet the value of much of this "counseling" and these "self-help" programs is dubious, for in claiming to have the answer, most counselors and authors are like the blind men meeting the elephant, each seizing one small part of the truth and claiming to know the whole. They have failed to heed Rilke's common-sense observation that true wisdom lies not in knowing the right answers, but in knowing the correct questions.

Shale Paul teaches us to ask the correct questions and suggests a practical way by which each of us can arrive at the correct answers for ourselves. He helps us to understand that until we grasp the wholeness of ourselves, it matters little how hard we work to control one part of ourselves or another. For such partial control leads only to inner war, one faction of ourselves contending furiously against another. We all know that inner conflict is dangerous to our health.

Such inner conflict is, in my view, the real Great American Tragedy. I have worked and bled with many thousands of Americans at that one point where the crisis usually strikes most severely—the maddening contrast between the way we think we must act in order to succeed in our jobs and careers, and the way we would like to act in order to save our whole lives. This is the horrible American dichotomy, the agony that is tearing so many of us apart.

Yet there is a way to resolve this dilemma. It is possible to reach the dynamic balance of one's own choice among jobs, careers, and life itself. It is possible to be completely practical about these crucial issues and still be at peace with everything else in our lives. Not, as the Valium culture tells us, by deadening our other senses, but by blending all of our sensibilities into one master design suitable to each of us as individuals. Strange as it may sound to western ears like mine, one practical way to achieve whatever each of us chooses is to view success in all things as *michi*, better known in Chinese as the

FOREWORD

Tao. Communicating on several levels—the level of obvious everyday phenomena, the intellectual, and for those who listen closely, the deeper spiritual level—Shale Paul leads us along this path.

I thank Shale for the gift of *The Warrior Within.* Unlike so many other recent works purporting to deal with our common anxieties and practical worries, his is not designed to turn us into savage infighters or jungle terrorists, each trying to outdo others in a desperate struggle to survive. No, *The Warrior Within* shows us how to become friendly giants, living comfortably and at peace with our work, our fellow humans, and above all, ourselves.*

JOHN C. CRYSTAL
1983

* *John C. Crystal is an internationally recognized leader in the Human Development field. An author, consultant, lecturer, teacher, counselor, innovator, and pioneer, Crystal originated the Life/Work Planning Process so well known in that field today. During World War II, he served as a U.S. Army Intelligence Officer in Africa and Europe. Later, for many years, he was an international business executive with several major American firms. He is now Chairman of the John C. Crystal Center for Creative Life/Work Planning, 111 East 31st Street, New York, N.Y. 10016. Crystal is co-author, with Richard Bolles, of a text on career/life planning,* Where Do I Go From Here With My Life.

ACKNOWLEDGMENTS

Authors are more recorders and synthesizers than creators. The fruits of their labors stem from seeds planted by others along the way. To those unsung heroes with whom I've been privileged to walk and sometimes compete, my gratitude goes out.

Special thanks are due those who patiently reviewed the manuscript that led to the completed work: Al Siebert, Tim Cameron, Barbara and Russell Brines, and Steve Blackwelder, for their careful reading and obvious caring; Mary Hey, for her thorough copy editing; my mother, Blanche, who shared her perspectives on our common experiences and to whom this book is dedicated; my daughter Jen, for her objective criticism and continued positive support; my son, Ken, for his efforts in the art department; my wife, Carol, for her forbearance in accommodating the unusual paths my life has taken (living with a warrior is not always easy); and her father, Erwin Canham, whose critical observations spurred me on.

Finally, I want to thank my aikido instructor, Koichi Kashiwaya, and his wife, Erin, for their help in bridging the gap between the Japanese and English languages and ensuring that the necessary nuances of meaning were reflected in choosing the frontispiece characters.

ACKNOWLEDGMENT

INTRODUCTION:
THE WARRIOR'S WAY

Who is a warrior? Ask ten people and you'll get as many answers—a Chinese ruler, an Indian chieftain, a samurai. Names like Genghis Khan, Geronimo, and Miyamoto Musashi crop up, men of great daring and purpose who were sometimes ruthless and cruel. These are the traditional conceptions.

Miyamoto Musashi illustrates the historic warrior. Born in 1584, he became one of Japan's most famous sword fighters. He fought more than sixty contests before age thirty and killed all of his opponents. He became so invincible that he continued to win when armed only with a wooden staff against steel swords. He retired undefeated and went off for twenty years to meditate and write his famous treatise on the principles of sword-fighting, *A Book of Five Rings*.[1]

Musashi wrote about more than sword strategy. He turned his cutting skills inward in a rigorous self-examination of the warrior's way. In explaining his use of *michi*, (the Way), the translator noted that "it is equivalent to the Chinese 'Tao' and means the whole life of the warrior . . . the road of the cosmos, not just a set of ethics for the artist or the priest to live by, but the divine footprints of God pointing the Way."[2]

Musashi regarded sword play as a key to life itself. He sought to extend the strategies of combat to all human interaction and, in so doing, failed to perceive two vital points: (1) that martial and physical force are only shadows of true power, often impressive but always specious, and (2) that all strategies—even those in this book—are temporary. Like many warriors before and after, he allowed himself to be limited by his experience and his predilections.

I have chosen the warrior metaphor because it fits my own

---

[1] Miyamoto Mussashi, *A Book of Five Rings*, trans. Victor Harris
[2] *Book of Five Rings*, page 34, footnote 1.

life, but I have expanded the concept far beyond its traditional meanings. My warrior unites with those fierce fighters of the past principally in the intensity of commitment. Beyond this, their paths differ markedly. The intent of **this** warrior's life is self-discovery rather than conquest. This warrior is not so much a single person as a state of mind, a consuming commitment to find his or her own inner truth and live by it. My warrior may be male or female, short or tall, or wear battle gear, a gray flannel suit, or a blue dress. He or she is distinguished not by physical strength or outer garments, but by inner direction and purpose.

The warrior philosophy as presented here is not simply a distillation of various eastern and western ideas, or a gimicky how-to-become-enlightened handbook. It is a process that can lead you back to your self and to the source of all things, individually perceived. It presents an apparently logical approach that gently allows you to return to the realm of original thought. The concept is perhaps best illustrated by the Japanese characters shown on the front cover. The top two, *ken sei*, may be translated as "saint above the masters." The lower ones, *sho hon*, mean "the essence of the source." Implicit in them is that the warrior spirit ultimately takes one above mentors and external authorities, and leads inward to truth itself.

The warrior spirit and concept, once grasped, act as a telescope to focus the energies and unite thought and action in a single, all-encompassing goal of self-discovery. Discovery is an important aspect of the warrior spirit, for it leads to responsibility, being responsible for oneself and **to** others, but not **for** them. The warrior's way leads to true power, dominion over one's experience and confidence in its significance.

Not everyone wants to be a warrior. The concept and philosophy of warriorship are demanding and unyielding, but the rewards are inexplicably great. For many, external rewards and the loving support of others is sufficient. For others, perhaps you, the reader, there is a nagging feeling that nothing less than complete self-awareness and understanding will do. It is to you, the seeker and would-be seeker, that this book is addressed.

The book is both an explanation of the warrior philosophy and a manual for developing—or rather discovering—the war-

rior spirit in yourself. It outlines approaches for radically alter-
ing your life patterns in ways that encourage your own self-discovery. The course it recommends is demanding, so you may
want to approach the subject piecemeal, that is, sampling a bit
here and there, digesting what seems to be useful and relevant
now. That's fine. Many of the changes you'll experience will
take place gradually over time, often without notice. And the
parts that are important for you will become apparent as you
read and experiment for yourself. I would caution only that
you not be surprised or alarmed when you find yourself changing in perhaps unusual ways. That is part of the discovery
process.

The book begins with a brief description of an event that
triggered the process in my own life. "Canyon Junction," the
first chapter, tells of a raft trip down the Grand Canyon in
which spontaneous discovery became an obvious alternative to
other ways of learning. Chapter 2, "The Constructed Self,"
takes a different course as it describes the reactions that cause
us to be captured by our experience and controlled by our own
self-imposed reactive patterns. This chapter reveals the dilemma
in which we all find ourselves at one time or another.

Chapters 3 through 6 are method chapters that offer specific exercises for awakening the warrior spirit in yourself.
Chapter 3, "Sensing Direction," describes the why and how of
writing your own history and suggests autobiography as an
excellent way to view yourself and your life more objectively.
Chapter 4, "Finding the Center," defines the center and tells
how it and you are related to real and apparent power. This
chapter is crucial to understanding the techniques presented in
chapters 5 and 6, "Tuning the Mind" and "Tuning the Body."
These chapters are designed to help reestablish the partnership
between mind and body that so many of us seem to have lost.

There is a distinct difference in tone as you go on to chapters 7 and 8. Most of us are fairly comfortable with logic,
having been raised in a world where reason and argument are
generally regarded as superior to feeling and intuition. Chapters 3 through 6 build on that comfort. They take you gently
from a place where logic is primary to one in which your
respect for intuition **and** your intuitive capacities are greatly

INTRODUCTION

increased. In a sense, these chapters use logical approaches to overcome the limits of logic. So, while you'll probably be comfortable with the reasonableness of the techniques presented, you will have to have some faith, because I've hinted at where they will take you.

Chapter 7, "The Discovered Self," presents the warrior philosophy in terms of eight qualities that make up the warrior self. These qualities reflect a deeper perception of the reality of one's self, and lead naturally to twelve strategies designed to protect and nurture the discovery process. The strategies are essential to the warrior philosophy.

Finally, chapter 8, "Discoveries," more personal in nature, consists of six short vignettes about ideas most of us think about from time to time, such as succeeding, competing, loving, and dying. The pieces, with some editing, were lifted from a personal journal I've kept over the past decade. They reveal where I am now, but not where I may be tomorrow. The final one, "Return to the River," concludes with a gentle tentativeness that seems appropriate to the warrior philosophy.

The reader should be warned. This is not a book to be read quickly and mastered easily. The techniques are presented clearly and methodically, but mastering them will require your diligence, inspire your doubt, and call upon your faith. You will find the journey invigorating and, like anything else really worthwhile, demanding.

One more caveat. This book is based on experience rather than others' research or quoted authorities. The anecdotes used have been drawn from my life and from the lives of others I've met while giving seminars throughout the country on personal effectiveness. I have drawn upon more than twenty-five years as a business executive and entrepreneur, nearly twenty years in the esoteric aspects of three martial arts, and an exciting array of "highs" as a pilot, athlete, husband, and father. While the specifics are mine, I think you'll find there is a universal ring to them that connects us all.

SHALE PAUL
May, 1983

CHAPTER ONE
CANYON JUNCTION

Augustt, 1972. Three jobs, eighty-hour weeks, high-pressure days, and Carol decides we should take a raft trip down the Grand Canyon. I was annoyed, uninterested, and concerned that the business could not do without me for ten days. Finally, I agreed to go.

We flew to Grand Junction, Colorado, and drove to Green River, Utah—a gas station, a cafe, and a motel surrounded by dust, sagebrush, and high winds. The flight was pleasant and uneventful, a mixture of new sights and scribbled notes, reminders of things to do when I returned home.

Dusk found us and twenty others with knapsacks and bedrolls in front of the motel, preparing for an early departure. We were a mixed group—a printer and his son from Chicago, a family of four from Pennsylvania, three or four other couples, some singles with varying hair lengths, and us. We had little in common except our destination. Our guides, Jim, Foxy, and Z, told us to be up at 0600 for a thirty-mile drive to the launching point.

We were to begin our journey on the Green River, follow its meandering course some ninety-five miles south into Canyonlands National Park where it joins the Colorado, and continue on to Lake Powell, another sixty miles downstream. Compared with the Ohio, the Monongahela, and the Mississippi, the Green is a muddy stream. Our launching was inconspicuous—two triple rafts, twenty-two novice rafters, and three seasoned guides—all viewed only by a skinny cow who was totally unimpressed.

We spent the first day matching names and faces, picking places to perch, and floating along in the water. I found a spot at the stern of one of the rafts where I could observe the

1

passengers and monitor our progress. My lukewarm enthusiasm had given way to mild curiosity as to what lay ahead. Looking at the gentle terrain through which we passed, it was difficult to believe we were headed for any kind of canyon.

Three days later we were submerged in 2,800 feet of sandstone and millions of years of prehistory. Sheer rock walls and narrow side canyons dwarfed voyagers and rafts alike. The impact was gentle, yet powerful. Each of us reacted differently. Some chattered nervously. Others grew quiet. Several pressed the guides for a lesson in geology, and one woman took pictures of nearly everything.

I was awed by the stark beauty of the canyon and, as it turned out, unprepared for its effect on me. We beached the rafts on a sandy shore for lunch. Carol and I climbed up on a high rock to eat our sandwiches. Gazing at the muddy current with its swirling eddies, I suddenly realized I hadn't thought about my business for two and a half days. I sensed a change in my mood, a turning inward. Carol noticed it too and asked as we resumed our journey, "Are you all right? You're so quiet."

"Yes, I'm fine," I replied.

My feelings deepened as the river fell. I sensed the presence of those who had gone before—Fremont Indians who lived in the canyon nearly a thousand years ago, outlaws for whom it was a place of refuge, Spanish soldiers on their way to California, and explorers bent on learning more of the canyon's secrets. Somehow, I felt a connection with those ghostly inhabitants, as though I had been welcomed to their land and, having entered, was being changed by it. The feelings persisted throughout the day.

We made camp the third night just after joining the Colorado. Behind and above were the Spanish Rocks, giant pinnacles that marked the Spanish crossing. Two of the guides offered to go with me on a climb. It was rumored that there was a hidden valley somewhere high up in the rocks. One of the guides had heard about it but wasn't sure of its location. We decided to set out and, with the three hours of daylight left, attempt to find it.

We climbed nearly 2,000 feet over decaying scree and up sheer rock walls, sometimes on goat trails, more often across unmarked terrain. Finally, we came to what looked like the top. Slips of blue could be seen through the rocks. Were we really there? What lay beyond? Would we emerge on a plateau or a razor edge?

We were stunned by what we saw. In front of us, extending for perhaps a mile, was a wide green valley surrounded by rock walls. We stood poised at the top, then ran screaming down into the valley floor below. When the echoes subsided, the valley resumed its silence. We continued on, each engulfed in his own thoughts. We found remnants of an early civilization—caves, wall paintings, and trails leading to still more caves and paintings. Yet we saw no living thing other than the lush grass of the valley floor.

I climbed to a cave overlooking the valley and paused, my mind filled with memories of the past—two fathers; a disjointed childhood; struggles with the religious truths of my upbringing; battles fought, won, and sometimes lost. My mind reviewed an endless jumbled series of events, like a poorly written story that badly required editing. As I stood there, I don't know how long, the pieces seemed gently to reorder themselves into a different pattern. I felt a deep sense of peace and a kind of breath-holding expectation, and knew that this subtle reordering of the past had immense implications for the future.

This sense of awe held each of us as we began the trek back. We hardly spoke for the first mile and began to converse openly only as we started our descent down into the canyon. We reached camp shortly before midnight to find the others concerned by our long absence. Fortunately, they had saved us a dinner of pork chops, potatoes, salad, bread, and steaming hot coffee. We ate ravenously, describing the trip between bites. We talked of the long climb, the valley, and the cave paintings but, as though by unspoken agreement, told what we had seen rather than what we felt.

The trip ended at Lake Powell, where we picked up a rented car and headed for our first night in a soft bed. We showered, rested, and watched a herd of deer from the motel window. I recall telling Carol, "I want to say this now so we'll both remember it later. Something happened to me in the

3

canyon that I can't explain. It's as though my past has some-how been rearranged and given new meaning. I sense that some inner process has taken over and is changing my life in subtle ways. I don't know what it means, but I'm convinced that things will be different from now on. It's as though I'm on the verge of understanding much about myself for the first time."

Subsequent events were to prove that early perception. In retrospect, the experience was a watershed, the beginning of a fundamental change in orientation. I still marvel that I accepted the experience without judging or doubting. My whole ordered, controlled way of looking at things changed dramatically in the space of a few days—or was it a few thousand years? And I felt comfortable about it. But why there? Why in the bottom of a canyon nearly two thousand miles from home? Why not in Virginia where I lived or on Cape Cod where I'd spent so many happy summers? And what next? Where would this strange vision take me in the future?

CHAPTER TWO

THE CONSTRUCTED SELF

It's been more than ten years since that trip down the Grand Canyon. Much has changed. I'm no longer a planner of corporate strategies, a condominium developer, or a homebuilder. Now I consult, write, and give seminars on personal effectiveness. I help people to experience life more fully, and I learn by doing it.

In my seminars, I've met many who have had similar experiences, turning points in their lives that pointed them permanently in new directions. But I've met others who've had no such highs, for whom past and present are burdens. They are victims—as I was until 1972 and for some time beyond—of what I call the constructed self, a vicious triad of impacts, reactions, and patterns that threatens to take over and govern one's life. I don't mean these people aren't successful. They are often spectacularly so. They hold responsible positions in their companies, have excellent incomes, and are active in their communities. But in their questions and discussion, they lift the lid a bit and reveal what's underneath . . . a sense of being driven by circumstance, not being fully in control, wanting more but not knowing just what.

Midway through a seminar one morning, the director of a large organization raised his hand. He had remained silent while his subordinates had participated actively. "Mr. Paul. I've listened to everything you've said the past two hours and I find myself agreeing with just about every word. But I want to say this. Do you realize you've undermined all that my church has taught me in the past thirty years? I see now that **my** constructed self is what the church has told me I am, and that it isn't true."

What is the constructed self? How is it formed and why does it seem to exert such control? Let's look at its component parts.

Impacts

We are born struggling, for air, warmth, milk, attention, and love. We're low man or woman on the totem pole. Everyone is bigger, stronger, and more sure. They know more and can teach us. We look to parents for guidance and support. If we lose a father or mother, it can be traumatic. At seven, I was confused when my mother divorced my father. I searched for the villain, someone to blame for my confusion and pain. I blamed "him" because he wasn't there. I concluded that your best friends, even your parents, can let you down, and I developed a cautious way of reacting to others' love, as though I were always standing a couple of steps away.

As a child, it's often difficult to understand. You want simple solutions, easy answers. You aren't sure who you are or what you want to be, and when the answers you get from adults don't make sense, it's easy to become frustrated. Disparities between preaching and practice are more felt than understood by the child. Their impacts can be both subtle and lasting.

We don't lack for mentors, at least I didn't. There are relatives, friends, and teachers, and each one has an idea about what's right for us. And, as if that weren't enough, we have the church and all manner of rights and wrongs. It's not that we don't have help; we have too much of it! We are taught rather than allowed to discover. Sometimes, even before birth, people have decided whether we'll be boy or girl, big or small, strong or weak. They've decided what college we'll attend and which profession is best for us. I had a friend in high school. His father, grandfather, and two uncles had been army officers. What was he going to become? Of course, a West Point graduate with an illustrious military career. That was before Korea and Viet Nam. Now he is a civilian. After ten years in the military, he found out that he could not follow in his father's footsteps, and to this day, he and his father don't talk about it.

Family, church, school, love, and marriage—how do they all add up? I spent more than three decades trying to put it all together. It was disconcerting to find that the simple answers aren't always the right ones and that authorities are fallible and human too. I was, as many of us are, conditioned to divide the world into neat compartments of good and bad, right and wrong, and I was uncomfortable when things didn't fit.

I learned to cope, happily for the most part, and I discovered that survival meant being able to react quickly and developing defensive patterns, walls of separateness to insulate me from them.

Reactions

Reaction is a way of coping. It's an automatic impulse often based on questionable premises and predetermined judgments regarding the outcome. In our society, reaction is a respected quality. Fast reactions are essential in most sports. The sharp rebuttal or sudden blow wins many a point in argument. The ability to react quickly to business setbacks is the mark of a successful entrepreneur.

You learn to react early when you begin life on the defensive and have to come to grips with much that doesn't add up. Reaction and defensiveness become habits that often carry well into mid-life. It took me years to fully comprehend a minor incident that occurred when I was fourteen. My mother remarried, and we moved from a small frame house on two acres to a huge estate with twenty-five acres, four houses, and assorted lawns, orchards, and pools. My stepfather, a successful developer and builder, had just bought my mother a television. He and two workers were installing the antenna when I appeared. In my excitment over the TV (our first), I shouted, "Gee Dad, that's really neat." He spun around to face me and said sternly, "Well, it's not **yours**." My eyes filled with tears. I turned and silently walked away, resolving that no one would ever hurt me like that again. It was years before I understood his motive, that he was learning to accept a marriage that included a built-in fourteen-year-old son.

Reaction can take many forms and produce varied results. Show fear and you'll lose face. Express anger and you may hurt those you love. Grieve and you can become immobilized with self-pity. You can seeth with desire, blush in embarrassment, boil with indignation, or be revolted in disgust. In any case, you're out of control, driven by the situation, hurt, and overcome by superior force. Whatever its form, reaction results in a loss of power. It allows circumstance to dictate. Yet we train and are trained to react quickly and repeatedly.

Patterns

It's natural to develop habitual patterns that allow you to react quickly, almost without conscious thought. For many of us, those patterns are keys to survival and success, planned forms of defense and attack that limit our vulnerability and make us more formidable. But all patterns will ultimately be found to be negative and binding. They promise freedom and deliver servitude. I recall a director in a large consulting firm in which I worked. He had quit college after only a year, convinced he could do better on the outside. He became a successful equipment salesman, served in World War II, and later joined the consulting profession. He had a razorlike mind, could spot a single error in a thirteen-column spread sheet in seconds, and could just as quickly understand a client's financial problems. Yet, when the going got tough, he would fold. In private conversations, he repeatedly apologized for his lack of education, and in client negotiations, he sometimes retreated as though afraid that the client might discover his secret.

For many of us, our adjustment to life is governed by such patterned reactions. I assumed the position of parental authority in our family for many years. We held "board meetings," usually around the dinner table after supper. That was the time and place for each child to bring up problems, raise issues, and ask questions. After suitable discussion, we would vote. Regardless of the numerical outcome, my vote always carried, that is until sometime after the canyon, when I stopped voting.

What can you do when you awaken to the fact that you are letting patterned behavior control you? Frequently, you react and develop still more patterns. I resented having to wear the tie, garters, hat, and conservative suit of the consulting profession, yet I thrilled to the challenges of solving client problems. I finally reacted, tossed it all, and took a job where I could do my own thing. Being a nonconformist worked for a while until it too became a pattern. Then I found it wasn't working, that in every organization there is someone to be accommodated, always the prescribed dress, the acceptable position, and the preferred style. Again I chucked it, traded a dark tie for an open-collared shirt, and became an entrepreneur. I escaped one form of conformity only to become subject to others—creditors, lenders, interest rates, even the market itself. Both gains and losses came in bigger chunks.

It's often difficult to avoid patterns that seem to work. My stepfather was successful by most measures—aggressive, wealthy, assured, and singleminded and intent on amassing millions. It was easy to accept his goals as my own, in part at least. I patterned my life after his and aimed for the top with his blessing and support. Only years later did I discover that those directions were inappropriate for me.

Patterns take many forms—bitterness, guilt, resentment, resignation, belief, disbelief, conformity, nonconformity, obedience, disobedience, and so on. Let's look at the first two.

Bitterness. At a time when most men retire, Dad bought the family farm about seventy miles from Pittsburgh. He built a twelve-acre lake, surrounded the original house with a larger structure, added a caretaker's house, and set about recontouring the fields and building new fences. Unobtrusively he acquired other farms, with an eye to making the entire valley a luxurious executive retreat.

Then fate and Pennsylvania politics took a hand. State officials decided the valley would make a nice park and fishing area. They began acquiring smaller parcels one at a time. No fanfare. No public announcements. Just the powerful acquisitiveness of a public agency armed with taxpayer funds.

They came to Dad last. No, he wouldn't sell. Then the state would sue, take the property by eminent domain "for the public good." Dad was furious. He fought and lost. The state acquired the farm, turned the remodeled farmhouse into an office, and began to flood the valley. Dad's dream became a nightmare of bureaucracy at work. He had confronted graft and corrupt politicians before and had little faith in the outcome. He eventually lost, not only the farm, but his health and his life. In the midst of the battle, he suffered the first of two strokes. Only after his death did we learn of the first stroke from a close family friend.

Bitterness slowly destroyed him. A tower of strength and confidence became an old man in a wheelchair. He survived for nearly five years after the earlier attack, but they were years of anger, of trying to get back, and of attempting to prove he could still win.

Dad's case is not unique. Increasingly, people today feel betrayed, taken and damaged beyond repair, for many reasons— Viet Nam, the economy, big business and bigger government, or fate. The reasons are unimportant. No matter who is the villain or what the event, we cannot allow bitterness to take over. When we do, it becomes a cancer that consumes mind and body. To give in and become bitter is to mistake effect for cause and to remove oneself from access to higher power. Bitterness is an admission that we are out of step and time and powerless to act.

Bitterness offers no solutions, only certain decline and demise, the prospect of being consumed by one's own constructed reality. The person who accepts bitterness into his or her experience gives away life and power needlessly.

Guilt. Few forms of patterned behavior are as deceptive as guilt. Guilt is a weapon with subtle and lasting effects. The director in my seminar hadn't recognized the guilt he had accepted until it dawned on him mid-morning. I learned how guilt works from a hired hand who worked on the estate grounds. We had bred my German shepherd and offered him one of the pups. He trained the dog by shouting at it, jerking its leash, and kicking it. Within a few short weeks, the dog's behavior became totally predictable. When his master approached, he would cower, head down and tail between his legs, awaiting the anticipated punishment and unsure of what he had done wrong. He, like many people, became perpetually guilty for crimes unknown.

Guilt arrives early and stays late. I watched a mother and child walking in the park. The child lagged behind, running from one edge to the other of an eight-foot-wide path. She called to him, "Michael, come here." The child stopped, looked at her, started forward and then halted as a brightly colored maple leaf fell to the ground at his feet. He stooped down and stroked its smooth surface gently. Suddenly, his mother was upon him, jerking him by the arm and screaming, "When I tell you to come, I want you to come immediately. Do you hear?" Tears streamed down the child's face as he was hauled away.

Guilt is most often, as in the case above, presented as necessary good. We are made to feel guilty so that we will conform, refrain from wrongdoing, and behave in a certain way. When we accept guilt, we are always acknowledging we have acted or thought wrongly. If I can make you feel guilty, I can control you. If, in addition, I can convince you that I have the answers, you will follow me.

Nowhere is this masquerade of manipulation more apparent than in organized religion. Nearly every religion has its truth, which its adherents regard as unique, infallible, and final. And often this truth is sustained by threats, some overt, others hidden. Frankly, starting out with "thou shalt not" is the surest way to make me want to. And telling me that your position gives you some special power to define and forgive my sins makes me doubt both your intelligence and your veracity. If every religion has its truth and they're all different, we're in trouble.

We are often caught in this battle of absolutes. We strive to do what's "right," when we aren't really certain what right is. Oh, we know what we've been taught, but often this conflicts with the way we feel. A couple came to me, deeply in love and distraught by the advice given them by a senior member of their church. They had been warned that "sexual relations are only for the purpose of procreation and not for recreation." They were deeply emotionally and physically in love, but they felt they would have to separate because they could not uphold their church's position and remain together. What happened? Well, today they are happily married, have two children and, incidentally, belong to a different church.

Guilt generally does more harm than good. It is too often a club for the leader and a crutch for the follower. It is part of the constructed self that is imposed on us. We are admonished to hear the word and heed the warning or pay the price for violating truth that's been defined for us. We become afraid, guilty, and frustrated that this truth and our inner voice are at odds.

"But," you say, "isn't guilt sometimes a good thing? Isn't it sometimes the only way some people will change?" Consider this. If your son makes a mistake in an algebra problem, do you make him feel guilty or do you help him to see the correct approach? Guilt is always opposed to clarity of perception. Guilt and fear combine to paralyze. At seventeen, I recall freezing to the stick of a J-3 Cub when my instructor screamed at me for failing to keep the plane on a straight course. We forget that even if people are guilty, their guilt stems from misconception, an inability to see clearly. The task is to help them gain clearer perception, not berate or frighten them. Guilt and clarity are irreconcilable.

I hate to admit it, but I have trouble finding God in church. I've tried, but I find the words too fast and the truth too pat. I don't **feel** guilty and I don't like to be preached at. Don't get me wrong. I'm not against words. It's just that I move at my own speed, and when they come from the pulpit, they often go over my head. I need to get off by myself, think about things, and listen quietly to what's inside. I'm more comfortable sitting on a rock than in a pew. There, the wind and the sun have a message for me, and it's **not that I'm guilty!** Much of the time, I feel a deep sense of love. I choke up when I see someone "running" a marathon in a wheel chair or watch a mother caring for a retarded child. My eyes get teary and I wish I could bear part of their load. I have so much. I can walk, run, see, hear, and feel. Who wouldn't be grateful to God, in my position? I don't know why I can run and someone else can't, why I have four limbs and others three or two. But I want the right to find out for myself. I want to discover and share the spontaneous joy that lies beyond guilt, anger, and patterns.

Styles

Bitterness and guilt are but two of the patterns of the constructed self. Far more common, though perhaps less obvious, are patterns contained in the styles we assume—parental, managerial, amorous, and social. People adopt styles for many reasons—to gain a sense of identity, to avoid feeling awkward with others, to get ahead in a particular job. Style is a kind of conformity. It is the *reductio ad absurdum,* the ultimate foolishness in patterned behavior. Styles allow us to substitute reaction for thought, defensiveness for caring, and certainty for truth. Kindly negotiators can be just as fake as ruthless dictators. They are just less obtrusive about it. They make a fetish of being fair and seeking consensus yet often exhibit the patronizing sanctimoniousness of a preacher angling for a Sunday dinner.

Reactions, patterns, styles are all crutches to support the constructed self. We're afraid to reveal our humanness, our vulnerability. In our quest for security and certainty, we become involuntary hypocrites, paper people and partial performers. We put off and frighten those around us and force them to react. We drive them into their own patterns. A middle-aged couple attended one of my seminars. He was surly, ugly, unpleasant, and had quit trying, and admitted it. She was soft, fragile, and hurt, resolved to stick it out with only occasional and feeble attempts to fight back. Together they were engaged in an undeclared war with nearly everyone—each other, co-workers, friends. Their lives were governed by patterns that he had created and she had accepted. They were fighting an endless round of competitive reactions.

When I was busy being an authoritarian father and aggressive entrepreneur, I sensed it wasn't working. I wanted to take time and figure it all out, but I was too busy accomplishing. I wanted results. So I set goals, accepted overly simplistic values, and drove hard for success. By my mid-thirties, long before the canyon trip, I'd become bound by my own patterns, which were beginning to show signs of wear.

So I opted for the obvious solution: run harder, work longer, and retreat still further into the truths I'd been taught. Only it didn't work. The canyon caught me mid-stream, ready for a change of course and uncertain which way to go, but it convinced me that direction **can** come from within and that the right course is often at variance with the accepted truth. It was, for me, the beginning of the discovery of the warrior spirit within myself.

In retrospect, I'm not surprised that answers didn't come from others. I've learned that society doesn't help much. It places a premium on order, rationality, and conformity. It shuns feelings and intuition and demands that you be up and about, doing, achieving, and winning. Wherever you turn, there are pat answers, simplistic solutions, and moralizing lectures. It's no wonder people leave their churches and families and become workaholics or worse. They are, like our gardener's dog, victims of reactive patterns and unable to escape. They've lost the spark of spontaneity and are bound to the future and the past.

This sorry scenario doesn't happen to everyone, but it's common enough that it's worth asking what can be done about it. For those to whom it has happened, the need for solution is critical. Sometimes, the struggle is so intense that they just give up and give in to a life of painful mediocrity brightened only by the imagined joys of a peaceful retirement. More often, they keep on struggling, as though by effort alone they can win. They can't imagine a world without struggle or a life of inner peace. They learn to live with discontent and sometimes become willing, even eager, to pass it on to others. In such cases, it's easy to reach a stalemate, a time when there's nowhere to go.

Breaking the Patterns

It doesn't need to be this way. The patterns of the constructed self **can** be broken, transcended to reach new heights. How? Well, you might try rafting down the Grand Canyon, climbing a mountain, or any other off-the-wall venture that lifts you out of the problem situation. Your friends will probably tell you you're crazy and that it won't work, but it **does** work for some.

Or you might try failing. I am constantly impressed by people I meet who have been ennobled and invigorated by failure. To a man or woman, they are tougher, more buoyant, more fun to be with, and have an incredibly positive outlook on life. They have learned a single invaluable lesson: there is no such thing as failure; there are only lessons that haven't been learned.

If you're very lucky or blessed, you may be helped by someone else, not a teacher or mentor but someone who comes into your life almost by accident. He or she brings new questions, different challenges, another kind of understanding. The person raises your hopes, rekindles your passions, and inspires your efforts. If this meeting is less by chance than providence, you begin looking at yourself in new ways. You perceive vaguely and uncertainly at first (at least, I did) that there is within you a whole new set of qualities, a more complete goodness, and a more sure inspiration.

Whatever the catalyst, the sudden or gradual force that casts doubt on past ways, it's important to follow it up. In fact, once the inner voice beckons and you stop to listen, it's difficult to turn back. You are awakened, challenged, and driven to dig deeper. This is the warrior spirit within, that fierce indwelling force that puts self-knowledge above all else and regards life itself as a laboratory for self-discovery.

But what if you've had no canyon or mountain, no spectacular failures, and no special friend? Where and how do you begin? Who or what holds the key to the present? The answer: you begin with the past, the architect of the constructed self. Only now you are in control. You are the potter and the past is your clay. You retrace early paths without bitterness, fear, or resentment. You are storyteller, weaving your own tale. You write your own history, your autobiography, and in writing it, you discover that you are participant and observer, always in the mainstream of action yet standing aside to grasp context and meaning. The secret lies in the way you go about it.

CHAPTER THREE
SENSING DIRECTION

I first wrote my autobiography in 1974. I was involved in a condominium project 150 miles away, flying out four days a week to direct construction operations, when the bottom fell out of the market. Money dried up and sales halted. Within a week I cut the field crew by 75 percent, drastically curtailed cash outlays, and wound up with time on my hands, up to three days a week absolutely free. So I flew off to our summer place at the Cape to think things out.

I was tired of building, sick of the feast-or-famine swings in the construction industry, and wanted out. But there was still the project to finish and an ailing father to care for. What could I do? An answer of sorts came early one Sunday morning. The patio bricks radiated the sun's heat as I browsed through the *Boston Globe*. There, in the middle of the paper, an article caught my eye. "McLean, Virginia" it began (home for me then), and it told of John Crystal's work in career planning. I clipped the article, tossed it in my briefcase, and resolved to look him up when I returned home.

Two months later I found myself sitting in John's office. Would he consider a one-to-one course? Since I was still traveling three days a week, regular classes were out of the question. I needed someone to talk with. I wasn't out of work or looking for a job; I just wanted to decide what to do with the rest of my life. Ripples from the canyon still nudged against the exterior shell of my life. Reluctantly, John agreed, and thus began a friendship that endures to this day.

My first assignment was to go off and write my autobiography. "Tell it like it is," John said. Four months later, I returned with 140 pages of polished prose. What's more, I had learned a lot about myself in the process. As a ground rule for the exercise, we agreed that Carol could read each chapter as it was written but that she would not comment on the content. She stuck with it until the fifth chapter. Then one morning, she came into my office and said, "I know I'm not supposed to say anything and I won't, BUT, I hope you realize how fast your thinking is changing." I didn't. I had sensed underlying currents but was unaware how much they were reflected in the writing. Months later, I began to gather the pieces and see the threads that wove throughout the narrative and my life.

In retrospect, I know of no other way to have gained such insight. The process of writing, editing, and rewriting produced unexpected results. Seemingly unconnected events joined in surprising ways. The finished product had a natural synergy; the whole was infinitely greater than the sum of the parts.

Writing your own story isn't the only way to gain a sense of direction, but it's one that works. Importantly, the success of the project doesn't have to depend on anyone else. As author, you are captain, mapmaker, and helmsman. I found that the process:

1. Enabled me to relive my past with the advantage of hindsight. (As I became involved in writing, I found that past events revealed themselves much like an old, familiar movie.)

2. Helped me to discover what I do best and what I like to do best. (Happily, they turned out to be the same: writing, speaking, thinking, and living life fully.)

3. Revealed threads of continuity in my life that vastly overshadowed individual crises and stages (although I was unaware of them at the time).

4. Raised questions that would not yield to conventional logic and that, therefore, forced me to a different level of introspection, one in which intuition rather than logic prevailed.

Autobiography was, for me, the beginning of a process of intense self-examination. It wasn't a panacea. I still managed to become sidetracked in another sizeable business venture before settling on my present course. But writing my history gave me an important start. As a means of broadening self-perspectives, it has immense possibilities, and it fits well with other approaches we'll be discussing later.

But why start with autobiography? Why not launch immediately into some of the more exciting aspects of personal development? There are several answers. First, I've found that most people are comfortable thinking about themselves, and especially with respect to the past. So autobiography is an easy way of getting into the subject. As a practical matter, your work in this chapter and in the three that follow overlaps. You'll be working with your autobiography while you're doing the exercises outlined in the next three chapters. So they all go hand-in-hand. But the most important reason is this: the steps described in this chapter will cause you to ask questions of yourself that you're probably not ready to answer now. The answers will come later in connection with your work in chapters 5 and 6. But it is important to formulate the questions now, before experiencing the changes that will result from your later efforts. So let's look at the writing process itself.

Writing Your Own Story

It's good to start by recognizing that writing your life story is a solo activity. Others can help, but more often they only confuse. A guide, skilled in the techniques of autobiography, is helpful but not essential. You can do it yourself, relying on your own intuition and recollections and following a relatively simple structure. Allow a spouse or close friend to read it if you must, but caution them to keep their own counsel and not to question, criticize, or attempt to influence your conclusions.

You may be tempted to reach for files instead of memories and to quiz others about what "really" happened. Don't. What counts is what's in your head, not in dusty records or others' perceptions.

Getting started requires commitment. It's best to set aside a specific place and time to write. For me it was my study in the early morning. For you, it may be the den or a bedroom in the afternoon or evening. Whichever you choose, stick to it. Dedicate yourself, the place, and your time to the task. Get away from distractions and out of others' traffic patterns.

21

Dividing your life into chapters. The chapters of your autobiography should cover time periods that are meaningful to you. I found it worked best if each chapter spanned at least a year, but no more than four. High school, college, or an early job experience are examples. Whichever you settle on, keep overlap between chapters at a minimum with each one representing a discrete period. Include events that are important and meaningful to you, not necessarily to anyone else. It's your story and you're writing it. Don't allow anyone else to do it for you.

Structuring the chapters. There are certain items you will want to include in each chapter. Adopting a consistent chapter outline makes it easier to refer back later. I found that five divisions worked well and strongly suggest that you include them in your chapter design.

1. *Summary.* Begin with a brief narrative of the period to be covered. Summarize it as objectively as possible. Put down the facts and avoid judgments or conclusions.

2. *Responsibilities.* Describe, either in narrative or list form, the responsibilities you assumed or were assigned during the period. Do this for both your work experience and your years at home and in school. For nonwork situations, report those responsibilities you voluntarily assumed or to which you fell heir. Go back and think about and record them as clearly and concisely as possible.

3. *Achievements.* What did you accomplish in each period? What was important to you? It doesn't matter whether or not you made money doing it, or even if anyone else knew about it. If something you did was important to you, put it down. I discovered, for example, that my most important achievements had little to do with making money. I was proud of having written a book, become a competent instrument pilot, and earned a black belt in judo—not much to do with success in the traditional sense!

You may want to record your achievements in numbered paragraphs. That way you can pinpoint your entries more quickly in later readings. In any event, you should feel good about the achievements you record; they should give you a sense of a job well done.

You might ask why money and recognition are not significant measures. Sometimes they are, but more often they are too restrictive (unless you rob banks for a living). Others' opinions are often based on limited evidence, emotion, and prejudices about you as a person. Your judgment is what's important. It's as though a little voice says to you, "I don't care what anyone else thinks. This is important."

4. *Atmosphere.* As you recall a particular period of your life you'll discover things that are important but that can't be called responsibilities, achievements, or activities. These are things you **feel** are significant about a person or an event even though they don't fit into one of the other categories. Include them here, preferably as numbered paragraphs. Begin by describing each point as succinctly as you can, and then amplify the feeling as clearly and as completely as possible. For example, you might want to describe how you felt about your parents at a particular time, your emotions when they sent you away to summer camp, or your reactions to your parents' divorce. Include anything you feel is important that doesn't fit elsewhere.

5. *Activities.* Record extracurricular activities (civic, political, religious) and hobbies in this section. Tell what you did and how much time and energy were involved. In some instances, you'll have to decide whether something belongs here or in the Achievements section above. As a general guideline, if the accomplishment seems more important than the activity itself, then it belongs under Achievements.

This section can be useful in two ways. First, your activities may reveal what you enjoy doing as opposed to what you did to put bread on the table. On the other hand, if you find that you spent every night out at meetings during a particular period you may discover that you were simply avoiding unpleasant issues at home. In my case, I found that I had allowed extensive church work to substitute for thinking hard about my own personal values.

Using Your Autobiography

When you've finished your story, what do you **do** with it? Well, **don't** rush off to a publisher or to your friends with the expectation that they will want to read it. In most cases, they won't!

First, put the entire project aside for at least a month. Get distance between your history and you. Give your intuition a chance to process the material as only it can.

After a month, ask yourself, "Am I curious about what I wrote?" If your answer is "No," put it off a while longer. The time will come. Meanwhile, you'll be working on a disciplined approach to change, which will affect your perceptions enormously.

Reading it. When the moment finally arrives, sit down and read your story cover to cover and ask yourself these questions:

- What feelings do I get? Do I appear different in the book from how I've thought of myself? If so, how?
- Does any particular chapter strike me with special force? Do I have the feeling that I ought to think more about that phase of my life?
- Are there unresolved questions or issues that seem to pop into my head as I read?
- Are there directions I want to pursue that I hadn't thought of? Typically, these appear as sudden insights, something like this: "Gee that was fun. Why didn't I stick with it?" or "Yes, I've always wanted to do that." Note your answers to these questions as explicitly as possible. Don't be alarmed if you have more questions than answers. Often the questions are the most revealing.

When you've finished, go back and read like sections without interruption. For example, read all of the Summaries, then all of the Responsibilities, and so on. As you finish a section, ask yourself these questions:

- What is the balance between assigned and assumed responsibilities?
- Has this balance changed over time? If so, how?
- Does this bother me? Why? (Why not?)
- How did I perform in each case?

- Why did I do some things better than others?
- Which responsibilities really turned me on? Why?
- Do my achievements fall naturally into certain categories? For example, are they things that I've usually done alone?
- Do they tend to follow a particular pattern? For example, how many involve making money, directing people, or working with things?
- In my current job, am I doing the things that I do best? That I **like** to do best?
- If I ranked all of my achievements (do it!), what would the list look like? Which ones would be in the top five or ten? **Why** are they most important to me?
- What is common to all or most of the things I've included in these sections? For example, are particular emotions, such as expectancy, fear, or anger, repeated throughout?
- Do these entries suggest answers to the questions noted in connection with the sections on Responsibilities and Achievements?
- What do these sections tell me about the kind of person I am? About what I want to **be** or **do**?
- What threads are apparent? In other words, are particular values, attitudes, or types of experiences repeated at different times in my life?
- What activities did I undertake voluntarily and enthusiastically?
- Which ones did I take on because of a sense of responsibility or at someone's urging?
- Is there anything common to those activities that I was particularly enthusiastic about?
- If I compare the time and energy spent in those activities with the responsibilities identified earlier, is there a correlation? For example, did I take on outside activities at a time when my job or home life was not going well?
- If I look at the list as a whole, which things did I enjoy most? Why?

Pulling It All Together

You may well feel, as I observed earlier, that you've come up with more questions than answers. Good! Don't feel guilty, stupid, or self-critical. Just note them and realize that they can lead you in useful directions, later.

Put the whole package away—books, papers, and all—for at least a week, longer if you like. When you feel comfortable, curious might be a better word, go back to your questions and answers and:

1. Write down each question on a separate card or slip of paper. You can type them on an 8 ½" × 11" sheet and then scissor them apart if you like. Then, organize them with the most important and urgent ones at the top, and the lesser ones toward the bottom.

2. Now look at your answers to the questions under the Responsibilities and Achievements sections. What have you done or achieved that you are especially proud of? Are you doing those kinds of things now? If not, why?

3. As you study your answers, what would you like to accomplish in your lifetime that you haven't? This is a big question. Your answer may take five sentences or five pages. Write it down. Now STOP. Put aside the entire package for sixty to ninety days and go on with the exercises described in chapters 5 and 6. Do them for at least sixty days before returning to the material that follows in this chapter.

This approach is designed to make introspection work for you in surprising ways. It combines disciplined effort, minimal structure, distance, and supportive physical and mental change to give you greater access to the balanced use of intellect and intuition. This combination can significantly alter your entire orientation toward both past and present. You will be able to gain a sense of effortless control over, or rather conformity with, your life (The significance of this distinction will become apparent later.).

From History to Planning

A word of caution. You may have a sudden urge to take charge of your life, launch out in new directions, develop grandiose plans, and generally get **moving** on something. Resist it until you have finished this book and are well under way with the work outlined later. If you don't, you'll discover that many of the steps you take now will only have to be retraced later. When you've practiced the exercises in chapters 5 and 6 for a while (you'll know when you're ready), you can return to the task of converting your insights into practical plans. When that time comes, and it may take weeks or even months, you'll be ready to plan, but you'll do it much differently.

Before we go on, I want to say a word about planning and how to plan when you sense you're ready. I made a mini-career out of a position of planning director in the late sixties. I discovered that formalized planning can easily become a substitute for creative thought. Plans can become rigid roadmaps or ineffective props for poor managers. Much planning today is poor planning. It is inflexible, unimaginative, and divorced from the real world.

I like to think I've learned something since then. I certainly don't plan my life or my business the way I used to. I'm happier, I'm more successful, and I find a delightful compatibility between work and play. I do what I want to do all the time. My life hardly follows the Harvard Business School model, but it is happy, full, and constantly challenging. What is different now? Well, two things. First, my plans have built-in flexibility that reflects a basic change in my outlook toward life. I used to plan five or ten years out. Now, on a clear day, I plan for the next! I'm concerned much more with the present than with the future. I view the future more as a function of unfoldment rather than decision. I'm much more willing to let things work out and to rely on my own intuition. This took time. I didn't achieve it overnight, but I **did** achieve it by doing the kinds of things I'll be talking about in the rest of this book.

Which brings me to the second point. I plan much more creatively now, for one simple reason: I am more open to options. I found that you can increase your option awareness, become more sensitive to possibilities. What follows in the remainder of this chapter is designed to help you strengthen your capacity to discover options while, at the same time, providing you with a minimal planning structure. I'll leave it

27

up to you **when** to get started on it, but I strongly suggest that you hold off until you've worked on chapters 5 and 6 for at least a couple of months.

Planning Creatively

Everyone plans. You plan when you get up in the morning, select a suit or dress, or make out a shopping list. Some people plan everything. Their lives are models of programmed action. They don't have much fun and they aren't very creative, but they *are* organized. The question is not whether to plan, but how to plan.

The secret of effective planning lies in having the planning process complement your creative abilities. Most plans suffer from sterility. They are either too brief (no plan at all) or too detailed and, frequently, simply linear extrapolations of the past. A really creative plan can do wonders for you. It can trigger your imagination, expose hidden alternatives, and help you chart a flexible course for the future. By learning to plan creatively, you can (1) focus on what is really important in your life, (2) become prepared for those insights that expand your mental horizons and allow you to perceive new possibilities, and (3) rid yourself of routines that inhibit spontaneity.

The best planning results from a balanced use of logic and intuition. The task is to achieve that balance, to combine structure and spontaneity so that your intuition and insights are supported and expanded rather than ignored or suppressed.

How Is It Done?

If you've been involved in formal business planning, you may find it hard to avoid the stereotypical approaches of systems logic. You're comfortable with reams of data and precise timetables. In such circumstances, it's easy to confuse process and result. A plan is considered good simply if it is voluminous, complicated, and covers all of the bases.

It took me awhile to find out that good planning doesn't always follow the traditional wisdom. The most complete analysis doesn't necessarily yield the best results. The most specific goals are not always the right ones. And the most well-written

28

plan does not guarantee achievement. I still plan these days, but I do it differently.

I set goals, things I want to accomplish in the next five or ten years, and objectives, things I'd like to get done this year. I try to think how I'm going to achieve my goals and objectives. I also look back periodically to see if I've achieved what I planned to do. But from there on out, I don't follow tradition. My Monday morning quarterbacking isn't an exercise in personal criticism or self-praise. It's an attempt to look objectively at where I am compared with where I thought I would be, and to understand the differences. The things I do are designed not to criticize my past performance so much as to help me develop a larger perspective and see increased possibilities. In fact, much of my life now is concerned with discovering possibilities where others often see only impossibilities. My planning these days consists simply of disciplined objective observation and delicate adjustment of attitude and structure. I know what's important in my life, and planning helps me be attentive to it.

How Can You Do It?

The most important question is: How can you do it? How can you make planning work for you? There are several things you can do.

1. *Be a philosopher.* It's important to know what you think **now.** What is your philosophy of life? Why are you on this earth? What is your fundamental purpose for being? Think about it. Write it down in a concise statement. When you've finished, use it as a measuring stick to observe change in yourself. Don't be dismayed if you read it again months later and think, "This doesn't apply now. I've changed." That's what life is all about—change and growth. The point is that, in addressing yourself to the big issues of life, you've set a course that will be more meaningful in the long run, and you've developed an attitude that inevitably brings out the best in you.

2. *Dream impossible dreams.* More people start out with what they **can't** accomplish than with what they **can.** A little

bit of negative thinking goes a long way. Before you know it, you're a maze of limitations, each one reinforcing the other.

One way to jolt the constructed self out of its limiting patterns is to think of possibilities rather than impossibilities. Seriously consider questions that may seem absurd to you at first glance. Ask yourself, What would I do if I had a million dollars tax-free right now? What if I had five million? If I could travel anywhere in the world, where would I go? If I could live wherever I wanted, what city would I pick? How would I describe my ideal job? If money were no consideration, what would I most like to achieve in the next five years. Speculate. It costs nothing, and it helps to stretch your mind beyond its limits.

3. *Put your wishes on paper.* Write down all of the wishes you can think of, everything you would like to be, do, or have. Put each one on a separate 3" × 5" card. Don't be bashful. No one else need see your cards.

When you've finished, go back and rank them according to their importance to you. If you had to pick one, which would it be? What would be your second choice? Continue until you've ranked them all. Now look at them. How much would it cost to achieve all of them? How many really are impossible? Which ones do you really want? What sacrifices are you willing to make to attain them?

You may be surprised at your answers. Your wishes may not cost as much as you thought they would. Many of them may not involve money at all. Others may be attainable if you decide they're important enough, and a few may not be so attractive once you consider what they actually involve. One lady wished for homes in Florida, California, and Hawaii all at once! When she began to think about it, she discovered that what she really wanted was to be able to visit those places occasionally, **not** to be saddled with three homes to maintain and eventually divide among her children. She found she could visit and rent a lot more cheaply and easily than she could live and own. But until she put her wishes on paper, the idea gnawed at her for years.

Another use for your wish list is as a gauge of your own

change and growth. Pull out your cards and review them every year or so. Update them. You'll be surprised at how many things are not as important now as they once were. Why? Because you've grown in the meantime.

4. *Look ahead.* Reread your statement of philosophy and purpose again. Now sit down and list your goals and objectives in three groups. First, list goals you want to achieve in the next ten years. Then list goals for the next five years. Now narrow your focus and list objectives you want to accomplish within the next year. Don't put down thirty or forty items. You won't accomplish them all, and you'll become frustrated. Keep your list down to no more than four or five in each category. That's still plenty to do. Now put each item in priority order within its category.

These are your targets, but they are more important as a form of discipline than as ends to be achieved. They help ensure that you will continue to look where you have been, where you are now, and where you're heading.

5. *Hold a weekly staff meeting with yourself.* Once a week, take a few minutes to see how you're doing. Think through your objectives; see what you need to do during the next week to keep on track. Review the past week and see how you did. Write down half a dozen things you want to accomplish during the coming week.

In a typical management-by-objectives approach, this is about the time when self-criticism comes in. You begin feeling guilty about the things you failed to achieve. Now, instead of launching into a silly exercise of self-criticism, ask yourself these questions: Why didn't I accomplish all that I set out to do? Did I take on too much? Have I sacrificed other things that I know are important? Does the objective still make sense? If I've been resisting getting something done, is there a good reason?

Asking questions enables you to impersonalize your evaluation. It helps you to appraise your progress objectively and take positive action rather than giving in to negative criticism. It frees you to rethink and replan in light of changed circumstances, your own growth, and an increased awareness of what's important to you.

6. *Take two steps back.* Most of the time, we're too close to our experience. Even the weekly sessions are apt to push us over the line where personal pressure and stress impede our progress. It's a good idea to get away from it all at least once a year, maybe oftener. Take two or three days off and think about your life. Leave your plans and lists at home, with two exceptions. Take along your statement of philosophy and your goals (not your objectives).

Spend the first day or so thinking about your life, where you are and where you want to be. Don't write down everything that comes to your mind. Just let thoughts come to you in a kind of relaxed way. You'll remember anything that's really important. When you feel settled and comfortable, take a look at the papers you brought along. Are there changes or additions you want to make? Have new ideas come to you that you want to incorporate into your philosophy statement? Are you satisfied that you're moving along toward the fulfillment of your fundamental purpose? Ask these questions of yourself gently and without criticism. Let the answers come to you.

You'll find this periodic vacation from your problems is worth its weight in gold. Often, you'll reach sudden insights that have profound implications. Incidentally, I find that an ideal time for this exercise is about two-thirds of the way through a two-week vacation. That way, you're relaxed and still not concerned about getting back to work.

7. *Do crazy things.* I find that, no matter how careful you are, most of your goals will be ones that you can defend to your spouse or your boss. They make sense and sound good when you talk about them. But life can and should take unexpected turns. Often these spontaneous events are critical to your longterm growth. In other words, it's the unexpected that may turn out to be the most spectacular.

You can prepare the way for these seemingly coincidental events. Pick an activity that appears incongruous, something most people wouldn't expect of you. If you're athletic, you might try learning to play the piano. If you're a sedentary type, get up early in the morning and take walks in the woods. It doesn't matter what the activity is, just make sure it doesn't fit your normal patterns. I take on something new at least every five years, in addition to all the crazy things I do regularly! I've flown planes, studied Japanese, taken up photography, and begun climbing mountains. Such activities stretch you, make you more flexible and fun to be with. Nothing bores a wife so much as a husband who brings home only a full briefcase each night. Imagine her surprise if, instead, he burst into the house and said, "Honey, I thought we might take a Spanish course, because I was thinking we might go to Mexico next year!"

It helps also if you can go outside your primary field of interest. If you're an engineer, study up on modern art or read a good book on poetry. If you're a mathematician, take time off periodically to attend the symphony or a rock concert. Find friends who think differently from you. Try to see the other side of every issue you feel strongly about. If you normally eat with the fork in your right hand, try it in your left for a while. There are endless possibilities. The point is to develop a habit of expanding your mental horizons by changing little things in your life.

8. *Keep up with your life story.* Make it a point to update your autobiography periodically. Your kids may not care about it when you're gone, but it will give you a sense of continuity. You don't need to make it fancy, but it's a good idea to stick with the original structure summary, responsibilities, achievements). The act of continually updating your story and your philosophy helps you remain young, enthusiastic, and forward-looking.

Where Does It All Lead?

Writing your life history, learning to plan flexibly and creatively, and following the exercises presented in this book can change your life dramatically. You can gain a new sense of direction, make your moments and your days richer, and learn to approach life as an adventure. You can begin to focus on life's possibilities rather than being stymied by its apparent limits. This book will put you in touch with that innate, in-dwelling warrior spirit that makes life itself a quest.

The next three chapters lead to a deeper sense of self, the

discovered self. This is the self that begins at the center, your center, and expands outward. It is the motive force behind the discovery process, and the key to real power. We'll be discussing this center, or *hara*, as it's called in the martial arts, in chapter 4. Then, in chapters 5 and 6, you will learn how mind and body can be used to enhance the discovery process. We will be talking about physical and mental fitness, but in the context of allowing rather than forcing the mind and the body to perform at peak effectiveness. You will learn why fitness is essential to full awareness and you'll discover that fitness doesn't have to be a drag; it can be fun.

CHAPTER FOUR

FINDING THE CENTER

I asked a friend, a practicing psychologist, if there was any single trait common to all of his patients. He paused thoughtfully and then replied, "Well, many people who come to me for help seem to be outer-directed. They see themselves as controlled by others, battered by chance events, and prisoners of their situation. They feel that their problems are beyond their power to solve."

Most of us probably fit that description at one time or another. It's easy to be influenced by others, especially if they're older or more experienced. Chance and circumstance seem to play a disproportionately large role in our lives. Being in the right place at the right time, born with a silver spoon in your mouth or under the right star seems more a function of coincidence than design. Why was I born a WASP, eased into instant wealth at fourteen, and destined to follow my stepfather's footsteps for more than twenty years? I've been more fortunate than many—blessed with caring friends and relatives, a good education, and a strong body and mind. Yet I've felt this outer-directedness my friend talked about, this uneasy sense that my fortunes lay "out there" in the hands of others, and that I was often off-balance and trying to gain control.

It's surprising that these questions were never resolved within the context of my own cultural or religious upbringing. I was raised with a firm faith in God and a healthy confidence in the ultimate triumph of good, yet I traveled half way around the world for answers.

Ever since I was ten, I've been fascinated by martial arts— judo, karate, and aikido. At an early age, I was impressed with the seemingly effortless efficiency of judo and the astounding power of its practitioners. While still boxing at the YMCA and wrestling in high school, I resolved that someday I would study the martial arts. My first opportunity came at eighteen when I enrolled in a jiu-jitsu course taught by a former carnival strong man. His methods were crude but effective, and within two years I found myself teaching self-defense to private citizens and law-enforcement officers. Later, while stationed at Quantico, Virginia, as a Marine Lieutenant, I joined the Washington Judo Club. Several times a week, I made a sixty-mile round trip to study the "gentle way." The generous guidance of teachers such as Jim Takemori and Donn Draeger spurred me on. Training was hard and competition tough. I won the East Coast white-belt championship and was promoted to brown belt.

Judo was more than sport or self-defense. It was fast becoming a way of life. I sensed that beyond the physical principles of throwing, choking, and holding were deeper threads. I was impressed by the quiet confidence of the best teachers and the uncanny way they could anticipate my moves. I noticed subtle changes in my own behavior—an increased awareness of things around me, greater confidence in my own intuition, and a feeling that I was on the verge of tapping into some greater power. These changes continued as the months went by. I became obsessed with the need to learn about the more esoteric aspects of the martial arts.

West Goes East

In September 1957, I left San Diego for Yokohama aboard a Japanese freighter, the Kochu Maru. Three weeks later, I was met by Donn Draeger, who had returned to Japan earlier for what turned out to be a long stay. Donn had found lodging only ten minutes from the Kodokan (judo's world headquarters), two large, western-style rooms in a Japanese hotel whose sign bore the inscription, "1,500 yen all night, 500 yen short time." The building had been taken over by the American Army, partially westernized, and then returned to the Japanese. It housed half a dozen women who catered to the needs of American soldiers. It included private bathrooms (cold water only), huge radiators (never connected), and comfortable western-style beds. The price was right, twenty-five dollars a month for each of us.

Kodokan, then, was a large gray structure near Suidabashi station. The exercise floor was covered with tatami mats. The building was unheated and, in the winter, snow drifted in through large open windows.

Practice began at about four in the afternoon. Students came from schools, colleges, and many of the "machi dojos," smaller practice halls scattered around the city. Typically, I arrived after having practiced in the morning and again in early afternoon at one of the smaller dojos.

Fortunately, Donn, a fourth-grade black belt, was well-known throughout the martial-arts community. He introduced me to teachers (sensei) who specialized in various techniques and saw to it that my instruction was thorough and tough.

Typically, advanced students develop certain techniques in which they become especially proficient—hip or shoulder throws, foot sweeps, chokes, and locks. The key was to find and study under masters who specialized in the techniques you wanted to learn. In more than seven months in Japan, I studied under half-a-dozen teachers, all sixth-grade black belt or higher. Two of these men made a dramatic impact on me.

Osawa-sensei twice had been all-Tokyo champion and was a master of the double footsweep. He was 150 pounds of contained, violent power. Rumor had it that he had hospitalized two opponents in winning the championships. Donn suggested that I study under him, but warned that I would have to pass his test. The test, as it turned out, consisted of randori (free exercise) for up to twenty minutes, during which he would throw me so often and vigorously that I could scarcely stand. When I weakened, he would throw me to the mat and apply a hold or choke. As I lay there gasping for breath, he would gleefully ask, "Paul-san, how much do you weigh?"

"165," I would reply.

"Ha, I weigh only 150," he would laugh. After seemingly interminable minutes he would drag me to my feet and begin the throwing ritual again. Suddenly, he would signal the end of the practice with a quick bow and a *domo arigato* (thank you).

This ordeal continued for nearly three weeks. I quickly learned the difference between teacher and student. One afternoon, Osawa made an innocuous joke at my expense. I laughed to show him I understood. This seemed to infuriate him. He threw me repeatedly until I could hardly stand. Then, just as suddenly, he stopped, smiled ever so slightly, bowed, and said in perfect English, "Thank you."

I returned the next day wondering what new tortures awaited. Osawa arrived as usual, walked directly to me, and said "Now, Paul-san, we learn." With that he began to teach. I learned why his footsweep was so murderously effective and saw how he could beat much larger opponents. He was a perfectionist, lightning quick, extremely flexible, and able to attack from nearly any direction. An opponent had only to take a single step to be vulnerable. Osawa had a virtue many of his opponents lacked; he was relentless in his attack, never stopping until he or his opponent was thrown.

Nakabaiashi-sensei was different. Tall, late forties, typically dressed in a conservative three-piece suit, he was a model of decorum and courtesy. He had taught Air Force Special Forces personnel and spoke English well. Like Osawa, he taught by example, talked little, and adapted his action to the student's need. Unlike Osawa, he displayed a kindly gentleness.

One evening, after we had practiced for several minutes, he threw me in a large circling arc and I landed resoundingly on my back. Again and again he threw me, always with the same technique. I thought that I recognized the throw as one long relegated to ceremonial functions, since it had been developed in feudal days and relied on the weight of heavy armor for its success. Without armor, it was virtually impossible to execute against an unwilling opponent. I haltingly repeated the name of the throw in Japanese, really doubting I could be right. He smiled, nodded, and promptly threw me again. I was dumbfounded, for he could not have thrown me by strength alone, yet the power he displayed was just short of unbelievable. Try as I would, I could not thwart his attack.

One of the most amazing displays of power came at the hands of a westerner. While practicing at Kodokan one afternoon, I was approached by a tall Caucasian with white, flowing hair. He appeared to be in his sixties, wore a black belt, and spoke with a strong British accent. "Would you like to do some holding?" he asked. As we went down to the mat, he told me to apply my strongest holding technique. Years of weight lifting and wrestling had given me confidence and strength in matwork. I applied *kata-gatame*, a hold in which I sat beside him as he lay on his back, locked his arm alongside his head, and applied solid, crushing pressure against his neck and arm. Normally, an opponent has little chance of escaping a properly executed hold. He asked, "Are you sure you've got it now?" and promptly sat up! I found myself dangling in the air. He had lifted my entire weight as though it were nothing. It was hard to believe. He smiled and said almost in a whisper, "You must learn where real power is." I learned later that it was Trevor Leggett, head of the British Judo Association, a sixth-grade black belt, and a serious student of Zen.

It was becoming obvious that power was much more than strength, and that the amount of power had little relation to the size of the muscles or standard principles of leverage. Something I did not understand was at work, and Leggett had given me a clue. I had been confusing physical strength and power, regarding them as identical when it was fast becoming evident they were not.

Western and eastern conceptions of power are poles apart. We tend to equate power with tension, contracted muscles, and various kinds of force—physical, economic, cerebral, and military. Even in idiom, we speak of "mastering the elements," "beating the odds," and "taking charge." We are at war rather than in harmony with our environment. In contrast, the eastern mentality is attuned to the subtle relationships between human being and nature. Instead of struggling against the elements, there is a sense of flowing with them. The pattern is evident in history, philosophy, and in the martial arts. Many martial techniques are identified in nature's terms, such as "earth and heaven," "the crane," "the waterfall," "valley drop." The skilled martial artist mirrors this flow in every movement, moves without apparent effort, and often with unbelievable speed and a sense of timing that borders on the supernatural. Then physical actions become the outward face of the interior mental world, which, for the experienced practitioner, is one of great calm.

I was struck by differences in teaching methods. Accustomed to detailed instruction, questions and answers, and frequent reviews, westerners are often dismayed at being left alone to pick up whatever tidbits may be dropped by a senior instructor or doled out in free practice periods, usually in the form of repeated throws, each harder and faster than the last. The sensei teaches by doing; learning becomes a joint experience of mind and body, a discovery rather than an exercise in memorization. Skills and insights come gradually, almost without notice. Change is sometimes slow but deep and lasting.

Injuries are frequent for most serious students. I suffered four shoulder separations, pinched nerves, pulled ligaments, bone chips, sprained wrists, and broken toes. I learned that I was more likely to be injured when I relied on strength instead of technique and when I became tense and tight. I found that deep mental and physical calm were effective in minimizing injuries and overcoming pain. I had competed while injured many times, finishing contests only by taping a wrist or ankle so tightly that I could not feel the pain. I wondered what would happen if I were confronted with a competitive situation when I was seriously hurt or ill. I had an opportunity to find out.

Shortly before leaving Japan, I was to be tested for black belt. I had competed in other clubs and had been promoted to nidan (second-grade blackbelt), but the real challenge was to be promoted at Kodokan. The exam was a high point, a privilege granted only by nomination of one's instructor. My test was set for the last scheduled competition before I was to leave Japan. It was imperative that I be ready. Two days before the exam, I came down with the flu, passed out, and was carried to bed. I slept, unaware of time until I was awakened by a voice, "Shale, you must get up. Your test is today."

The black-belt test includes a written examination on philosophy and technology; demonstrations of various throws, holds, chokes, and dislocation techniques; and a contest in which the student is matched against five opponents. He or she is given a minimum amount of time, usually ten to twelve minutes, to throw all five. Typically, the first two will be below the student's present rank, the third of equal rank, and the last two a rank higher. The objective is to beat the first three decisively, win against the fourth, and either win or draw the fifth.

I dressed and presented myself to the examining board—six instructors, all sixth grade or higher. Though still feverish and weak, I managed to get through the written and technical parts and now faced the competition. One of my instructors sensed my discomfort, took me off into a corner, placed a small brown folded paper in my hand, and whispered, "Take it, Paul-san. It will make you strong." My stomach was already queasy and I feared that eating anything might have disastrous results. I took the paper, slipped it in the folds of my jacket, and later disposed of it. Subsequently, I learned that it contained ground rattlesnake rattlers, a legendary strength potion!

I beat my first two opponents easily, using foot sweeps to conserve strength. The third and fourth were more difficult, but I took both with solid clean throws. The last was a tall powerful nidan whom I had seen in earlier contests.

We bowed, closed, and began moving around the mat, probing and testing. I had little strength left and felt that if I didn't make it on the first try, I would probably lose. As we moved, I sensed a weakness in his style, one which fortunately rendered him vulnerable to my strongest throw. *Uchimata*, or "inner thigh," as it is called, is performed by turning in to the opponent so that you are both facing the same direction and simultaneously lowering your body so that your opponent straddles your thigh and is drawn tightly against your back. You then do a somersault in the air with your opponent held tightly against your back. The beauty of the throw is that, beyond a certain point, it is nearly impossible to stop.

I turned, spun in, and stopped. I had come in too high and given him a chance to defend against the attack. Somehow, I regained my position and moved in again. This time it worked. We became airborne in a large arc and landed solidly. I won the match and my black belt, just three weeks before leaving for the States.

Power and the Center

I learned much about power from Osawa, Nakabaiashi, and Leggett, and from countless matches fought in Japan. I became convinced that our western ways were sadly misguided and resolved to continue my studies beyond Japan. I returned to Pittsburgh and continued to compete and teach, but gradually became absorbed with the family business. Judo practice became a weekly rather than daily event, and work and family took precedence over inner growth.

While in Japan, I had also studied aikido, an art in which the mental aspects of power are emphasized even more than in judo. Aikido differs from other martial arts in several respects. It is concerned with the unity of physical and mental action as facets of a single event. It aims at uniting and redirecting the opponent's power rather than blocking it. And it teaches the student to combat multiple opponents rather than a single adversary. Demonstrations of power by top aikido masters occasionally border on the supernatural.

I stood beside the mat watching an old instructor with long gray hair and a flowing beard. He stood calmly while ten assailants charged. He threw them easily in all directions and, in the motion of throwing, appeared totally calm. In the seconds of the melee, he was a blur. My eyes could not follow his movements. Then suddenly, he was there, still, in the center of the mat, fingers touching lightly and body motionless. No one, not even his assailants knew what had happened. They had attacked and lost. He had not attacked and won.

The key, he explained later, was to develop an inner stillness so complete that it became impervious to outer forces. And the stillness, he said, lay not in the brain or the muscles, but in the center, the *hara*. He said you had to **feel** it deep down inside. He talked of *kokoro-no-mizu*, "a mind as water," that is, one without conscious thought. In this mind, he said, one observes without judgment or reaction. He said that this calm stemmed from long practice and disciplined meditation.

His words came back to me long after I returned from Japan. I began to practice in ways alien to my western unbringing, sitting quietly for long periods with eyes half-closed and slightly out of focus, aware only of the rhythmic flow of my own breathing. Gradually, I became able to exclude all other thoughts. This practice continued sporadically for several years, then gradually waned. Again, after the canyon trip, I was drawn to resume meditation. I began meditating regularly once or twice each day.

My perceptions of people and things changed. I became more calm. "People watching" became a fascinating avocation. I felt as though I were looking beneath people's skins and behind their words. My sense of time changed too. I began to arrive at appointments on time with only a minute or two to spare, yet without hurrying. And I became more present oriented, less concerned with the future, and more receptive to inner leadings.

By this time, I had moved to Virginia, become a management consultant, and substantially discontinued judo. A friend invited me to practice aikido at a club chartered by Dr. Koichi Tohei, a world leader in aikido. I practiced for more than two years and had several opportunities to study under Dr. Tohei. He taught and demonstrated the power of the *hara* in dramatic ways.

We were in Greenwich Village, giving a demonstration to several hundred people at a local high school. Dr. Tohei agreed to pose as victim while his assailant, a third-grade black belt, charged with a short-bladed wooden dagger. On the initial charge, Tohei pivoted smoothly aside and, firmly grasping his opponent's knife hand, threw him in a large arc. Twice more his opponent charged, with similar results. Then, a fourth time, this one more rapid and vigorous. Tohei pivoted as before, only this time, he simply pointed his finger at the oncoming blade. Assailant and blade followed a circle traced in the air by Tohei's finger and landed resoundingly on the mat.

Dr. Tohei teaches that the *hara* is the physical and psychological center of gravity in the body. It's the place where everything balances. Physically, it's a point about two inches below the navel. Imagine running down a road and suddenly crashing headlong into a wire stretched across your path. If the wire were suspended at the level of your center, you would spin around the wire rather than tripping over it (if it were too low) or skidding to a halt (if it were too high). If you recall *uchimata*, the throw I used to win my black belt, you can now understand how the centering principle works. The aim is to get below your opponent's center. When you do, you can execute the throw easily, because you control your opponent's balance.

Tohei teaches centering in terms of four rules. While they

can be quickly grasped and easily practiced, their full significance becomes apparent only after you've practiced for a long
time. Here they are:

1. Maintain the one point.
2. Relax completely.
3. Keep weight underside.
4. Extend *ki*.

These four points incorporate the principles of centering in a
simple and effective manner. Consider each in turn.

To maintain the one point is to acknowledge mentally that
physical **and** psychological power emanate from the *hara*. Maintaining the one point is an act of mental decision that enables
you to develop and demonstrate this power. This doesn't make
sense logically. It must be experienced. If you haven't guessed
already, this reflects a fundamental difference between western
and eastern ways. Westerners want everything explained so
they can analyze and draw their own conclusions. Eastern
teaching, on the other hand, emphasizes a different kind of knowing in which body and mind share the learning experience, and
in which the student is taught to reserve judgment. He or she is
encouraged to observe and act, rather than question and criticize.
I suggest that this approach can be useful to you as well.
Accept the idea that power emanates from the one point (*hara*),
because such acceptance is crucial to a full understanding of
the true nature of power! Do you find yourself resisting? Well,
bear with me.

Tohei's second instruction is simple: "relax completely."
Why? Aren't loose muscles a sign of weakness rather than
strength? No. Muscle tension actually results in a loss of real
power although it gives the illusion of strength. The idea that
tension signifies strength applies only if you regard power as a
finite property of the muscles. Just for a moment, think of
power as flowing from an outside source, always in motion and
not limited to cells and muscles. This isn't too different from
current physics, in which all matter is regarded as energy, but
it goes further. Implicit in these four points is the idea that
power comes *to* us, that we are not its originators. You don't

have to accept my word. I'll show you how to experience it yourself in a moment.

"Keep weight underside," the third point, emphasizes that the heaviest point of any object is also its lowest point. We're all aware of this principle, but we continually violate it in our bodily mechanics by holding our bodies rigidly straight, walking in a forced manner, and constantly showing signs of stress in our body English. If you don't believe me, try this experiment. Ask a friend to stand with his arms at his side and command him to relax. Now reach down and lift his arm by grasping his wrist. Note how light his arm feels, much lighter than it actually weighs. Invariably, your friend will help you by anticipating your move and lifting his arm for you. If he were keeping weight underside, he would allow you to lift the full weight of his arm and would not subconsciously tense and raise it.

The fourth point, "Extend *ki*," requires some explanation. *Ki*, in the martial arts, means power, but not just physical power. The term includes mental, psychic, and spiritual power that must be experienced rather than explained. You can apply the concept and practice this fourth point **without** understanding it intellectually. Simply think of power (*ki*) as water coming from a garden hose, which you can direct by pointing the hose. Visualize this power as flowing from the one point through your body, down your arm, and out your index finger. When you learn to focus your concentration, you can then direct your power with extreme precision. Your focus, or *kime* as it's called in the martial arts, is your ability to direct tremendous amounts of power to a single point. Remember the extraordinary power exhibited by Osawa, Nakabaiashi, and Leggett? Those were illustrations of *ki* and *kime*—intensely focused power.

Does this sound odd to you? I'm not surprised if it does. It's difficult to appreciate the importance of these principles unless you've experienced them directly at the hands of a skilled teacher, but you can get an idea of the power they provide by performing a simple experiment for yourself. It is called the "unbendable arm" demonstration, and it's a standard test in aikido. Ask a friend to stand facing you, close enough so you can place your right hand on his right shoulder. Now make a fist, tense your arm up as tightly as you can, and ask him to bend it. Have him place both hands in the hollow of the elbow and gradually begin applying downward pressure until the arm bends. Be sure to pick someone strong enough to force your arm down. Ask him to notice how much pressure was required to bend your arm.

Now try it again, only this time, follow the four points. A good way to relax quickly is simply to shake your hands hard for a few seconds. If you have trouble focusing your attention on the one point, take your other hand and touch the point lightly with your index finger. Hold the finger there until you can clearly visualize it. Now begin visualizing the flow of power from the one point, up through your arms and infinitely out into space. Keep your extended arm completely relaxed. You may want to gently extend your index finger to indicate the outward flow of power. And, of course, remember that the heaviest part of your extended arm is its underside. Now ask your friend to apply gradual pressure as before and note the difference. You'll both be surprised. Your friend will find it is difficult if not impossible to bend your arm!

There's a variation of this test called "the unliftable weight." In this case, simply stand with your hands at your sides and ask a friend to lift you by putting his hands in your armpits and gradually applying upward pressure. The first time you do it, make yourself rigid, tense your muscles, and think up towards the ceiling. Now, the second time, apply the four principles. Again, you'll be surprised.

Aikido utilizes these principles in forms of holding and throwing with subtle but dramatic results. If you've ever seen Dr. Tohei in action, you know how powerful this relaxed kind of strength can be.

These exercises are not just parlor tricks. They are ways of demonstrating how power works when you are centered, that is when you are acting from the *hara*. To be centered, you must be in a relaxed physical and mental mode. You can practice centering in nearly everything you do. You can sit, walk, and even run in a centered mode, and you **should**! But you must practice constantly. Practice in centering strengthens the warrior spirit.

I taught this technique to the partners of an accounting

firm. After the session when we were preparing to leave, one of them came up to me grinning. "I just took my wife out to the car, and when I opened the door for her, I practiced being centered. And you know what? I ripped the door handle right off!" An unusual but by no means unique demonstration of the way power works.

Balance Is from the Center

Remember I mentioned earlier how I used to have a sense of being off-balance much of the time and of being controlled by others and by circumstance? Well, I've been practicing centering for several years now, and I've learned a bit about balance. There are two kinds of balance and both are necessary for full effectiveness.

Some time ago, I was in a doctor's office taking a flight physical, standing on the scales, the kind with weights. I adjusted them, first to the right, then to the left to get them level. It was surprising how sensitive they were. I could throw them off balance by curling my toes, rocking back on my heels, or by taking a deep breath. The scales represent static balance, very sensitive and easily disturbed. Many of us have this kind of balance.

There's another kind of balance, the kind you see in a toy gyro, the kind that derives its stability from motion. I've never outgrown my fascination with gyros. As a child, I would spin them and watch hypnotized as they stood still within their own velocity. Later, I learned to fly and navigate with their more sophisticated cousins, gyro compasses and horizons.

We need both kinds of balance, static and dynamic. It's easy to be composed when you're sitting in church or a quiet room. It's a good deal harder when all hell's breaking loose and you can't hear yourself think. Martial artists learn both kinds. Through meditation, they learn to recognize, in themselves, a deep inner calm. And through the constant challenges that are inherent in their practice, they learn to convert this static calm into a powerful imperturbable sense of dynamic balance.

Both scales and gyro reconcile opposing forces, adjust to multidirectional pressures. Scales are balanced only when they cease their seesawing and achieve a level stillness. The gyro is stable only when it moves and spins. The faster it spins, the more stable it becomes and the more motionless it appears. The turning parts are but a whir, but the outer frame is poised, calm, and linked to whirlwind speed.

We are both scales and gyro. We discover our balance in inner stillness and perfect it in outer movement. We can become the eye of the hurricane, the calm amid chaos. Unlike the gyro, we have greater capacity to adjust, to reconcile the subtle forces impacting on us and to impose harmony on apparent confusion. What is the secret?

We possess an almost infinite capacity to adapt, if we do not restrict it with our conscious minds. It is the power of dynamic balance. We gain it, not by resisting or retreating, but by combining and synthesizing, by the strength we draw from the world around us. We are process and purpose unified in the present. Spinning like a gyro, we develop our own centricity, our own freedom from position and dogma. This, too, is part of the warrior spirit.

The qualities of dynamic balance produce an aura of unpredictability, a sense of constant change and motion. We become inwardly flexible, bound by no pattern, and described by no style. We defy labels. We ascend above society's myths and histories. We become our own person, finding peace with the outer world in a dazzling display of motion.

How can we develop this stability? We begin in the stillness of the inner self. We listen until we are able to hear, until we no longer fear the inner voice, and until the signals become clear. We begin to feel the inner strength that dictates outer calm. Then we test. We begin with small challenges and look for proofs in seemingly insignificant incidents. We take our calm out into the world of conscious thought and action and periodically withdraw to recharge and rediscover. Then we go out again. This continuing cycle of rest and action, silence and sound, reveals the larger reality of which we are all a part. We begin to sense that our stability is a manifestation of a larger order, and realize that the nudges and jolts of the outer world are only parodies of true being. We learn to accept direction in small bits and make minute adjustments that leave us inwardly flexible and outwardly stable. We become perpetually centered and dynamically balanced and, in so doing, begin to understand the nature of real power.

Two Kinds of Power

Nearly everyone wants power. Athletes, executives, politicians, and generals crave it. All too often, however, they fail to perceive the differences between real and apparent power. This failure is the reason why so many people always search but never find.

Real power is innate and nonmaterial. It is discovered rather than developed. It is mental and spiritual—intelligence, mind, and love. Apparent power is a product of the constructed self and world. It is belief, reaction, brute force, and matter. It is nearly always derived from wealth, position, authority, or prestige.

Real power is perhaps best understood through metaphor and reversal. It is the dripping water that gradually wears away the rock. It is the profound silence that follows a high wind. It is the "still, small voice." It is the exhilaration of a new sunrise, a piece of music, or a loved one's touch. It is the loaves and the fishes that fed the multitude. Real power is like breath. It is experienced more in giving (exhaling) than in receiving (inhaling), and it must be experienced to be understood.

Apparent power is never what it pretends to be. It masquerades in borrowed forms, sometimes attractive, more often frightening. It promises and threatens. It thrives on fear, anger, will, and desire. Apparent power is **never** neutral. It is always negative, although it often assumes positive forms. Because it isn't neutral, it cannot be ignored, nor can it be combated with negative power. It's easy to spot those who have succumbed to the enticements of apparent power. They are, like the couple in the seminar, obsessed with controlling or being controlled. They may be ego-directed or outer-directed, but at either extreme, they are out of control. The visible signs run the gamut from irrational anger and frustration to a facade of benign pleasantness that masks deep hurt, fear, or remorse. Whatever the vesture, it all stems from being misled about the true nature of power.

51

THE WARRIOR WITHIN

Apparent power is always a misstatement, a misconception. It invariably attacks our greatest weakness and survives only by virtue of the reactions it provokes. It often seems to be more certain, attractive, and attainable than real power. It is the strength of position, the authority of command, the egotism of wealth, the force of will, and the conceit of self-praise. It is malicious in method and ultimately destructive to oneself and others.

The real strength of apparent power lies in the extent to which it is believed. And it can be believed only through misconception. For the person who possesses the warrior spirit, clarity is essential. He or she strives always to distinguish between real and apparent power, to use one and reject the other.

To gain real power you must stop, then begin again, return to the center. The center is the focus though not the source of power. We only think that power comes from position, money, or vitamins. In reality, it stems from our awareness that the centers of ourselves and the universe are one. It comes from harmonizing rather than mastering. The origin of power is the eternal, infinite, spiritual universe itself. The center within us is the lens through which that power is focused and intensified.

The person who discovers true power moves effortlessly, harmoniously, happily. Experience is unfoldment, problems are opportunities, and each day is a new joy. No person, thing, or feeling is trivial. No moment is unimportant, no day simply a stepping-stone to tomorrow. Power becomes a proof of congruence, a celebration of now.

When you discover this inner power, outward experience begins to conform. Things fall into place. People become important, each giving and receiving in harmonious balance. Taking, winning, and beating become irrelevant. Power flows, carries you along in a measured current of action, direction, and harmony.

With practice, this centered stillness becomes compass and gyro, guiding to new explorations of body and mind. We learn to open the mind and listen to the body, that each may become attuned to the inner processes of self-discovery.

Getting There

Remember I said you couldn't appreciate the full significance of Tohei's principles simply by logic? Well, this applies
to all aspects of centering, balance, and power. It's all right to
doubt, but you also need a certain amount of faith and commitment to succeed. An ancient Bhuddist saying posits these three—
doubt, faith, and commitment—as prerequisites for enlightenment.[1]

In the next two chapters, your doubt, faith, and commitment will be tested. I suspect you may be skeptical about the
benefits of some of the things I'm going to ask you to do. But I
trust that, having read this far, you'll have the necessary faith
and commitment to give them a try. If you do, you'll be well on
the way to making your own discoveries, and much that you
will read in the last two chapters will have a familiar ring to
your ears even though you haven't read it before.

---

[1]At first, it may seem odd to combine faith and doubt. Western religion
generally tries to dispel all doubt and requires sometimes unquestioning faith—in
the Scriptures, in a charasmatic leader, or in church dogma. Faith, doubt, and
commitment as I have used them and as they are employed in eastern
philosophies, are somewhat different. Doubt may be thought of as a healthy
and essential skepticism of all external authorities, a deep inner sense that all
truth must be tested for oneself. Faith is the certainty that proceeds from this
inner testing. Commitment is not so much will or dogged preserverance as
intention in action. It is the gentle, relaxed, and extremely powerful inner
motivation that results naturally from an awareness of the warrior spirit
within oneself. To one accustomed to making things happen, as I was for many
years, it can be both a refreshing and surprising change.

This combination of qualities is one with which most students of eastern
philosophy are fairly conversant. It is expressed somewhat differently by Miura
and Sasaki in their book, *The Zen Koan* (p. 42–43) as "the great root of faith, . . .
a great ball of doubt, [and] great tenacity of purpose."

CHAPTER FIVE

TUNING THE MIND

Brain is chemistry, physiology, physics, and biology. Brain is not mind. Mind is heart, spirit, soul, being. No English word encompasses the full range of mind. The Japanese word *kokoro* is better, more subtle, more inclusive. The *kokoro* mind is rich in the imagery of gentleness, wholeness, commitment, and sincerity. It cherishes, cares, knows, and remembers. The *kokoro* mind includes the whole range of conscious and superconscious being. It exists above and beyond brain. It ranges further, reaches deeper, and perceives greater possibilities. Brain seeks to exceed its own limits. Mind knows none. Mind is not concerned with reason and argument; it transcends them.

We know much about the brain, little of the mind. Scientists have studied shadow rather than substance. They've learned about the copy, but not about the original. Still, their research provides clues. By learning how the brain functions, we can discover how to overcome its self-imposed limits. The brain is our best friend and our worst enemy. It lifts us to soaring heights and plunges us into deepest gloom, all within the space of a few moments. To transcend it, we must know how it works.

Current theory divides the brain into two hemispheres. The left one controls the functions of logic, reason, and speech. It is linear and verbal. The right one is almost a mirror opposite. It is intuitive, spatial, nonverbal, and holistic. It knows rather than comprehends. It is aware rather than informed.

Reason and logic often lead us astray. How often have you wished you'd followed your hunches instead of accepting the "obvious" conclusions that seemed to follow from the facts? In many instances, we would be better off if we relied less on the rational left brain and more on its silent partner. Yet, most of the time, the left brain dominates while the right brain sits passively waiting to be called upon, occasionally warning that all is not right and generally being ignored. How can we learn to turn off the logic and tune in to intuition, or at least bring the two into balance?

One key may lie in the way the brain functions. We know that each hemisphere emits tiny electrical signals that can be measured in terms of cycles per second, or hertz. These frequencies vary considerably. When we're fully awake and alert, the waves are fairly fast, 13–26 hertz, and are called "beta." They slow down to about 8–13 hertz when we become drowsy or daydream. In these states, they are called "alpha." If we drift still further from the waking state, the waves decrease to 4–8 hertz and are called "theta." Finally, if we fall asleep, the waves drop to .5–4.0 hertz and are called "delta." Furthermore, these frequency changes are accompanied by changes in the character of the waves themselves.

More significant than the frequencies may be the relationship of the waves between the two hemispheres. In the waking beta state, they are asynchronous; that is, waves from the two hemispheres won't match when paired on a visual screen. It is only when they become alpha or theta that they match. This is the scientist's way of recognizing that, most of the time, we're unbalanced!

Brain and body are related in countless ways. The left side of the brain controls the right side of the body and vice versa, although this relationship is sometimes reversed in left-handers. The brain receives signals from nerve outposts throughout the body, monitors activity, and directs and redirects effort. The interchange is mutual. Brain controls body, and body influences brain. If we do something to the body, brain knows. There is even a connection between the way we breathe and the way we think.

Scientists have found that various physical and psychological changes accompany alpha-wave and theta-wave states. Heart rate, oxygen consumption, and carbon dioxide production decrease. Measures of galvanic skin response indicate reduced muscle tension. Blood pressure tends to normalize. Subjects in these states report a deep sense of calm, feelings of detachment, an absence of judgment, altered perceptions of themselves and others, increased sensitivity to sounds and colors, and subtle shifts in personal values.

It follows, then, that if we can learn to induce alpha and theta waves, we may be able to bring the logical and intuitive functions into an improved state of balance. What's more, it may take less effort, since altered states seem naturally to produce a sense of deep relaxation.

Remember I said there was a connection between the way you think and the way you breathe? You can test this for yourself. Sit quietly with your hands folded in your lap. Take a deep breath and hold it for about ten seconds. Don't count or wonder if you can do it. You can. At the end of ten seconds or so, exhale slowly through the mouth, allowing the breath to rise from the lower abdomen. Now, what were your thoughts while you were holding your breath? Chances are, you weren't aware of any. You were probably only conscious of an inner silence, devoid of thoughts. This stillness is significant. It suggests a way, which we'll explore later, of quieting the rational mind.

You may have wondered why I suggested that you put your autobiography aside after the question exercise. At that point, you were operating in a predominantly left-brain mode. You'll want to return to those questions, but not until you've learned how to achieve the kind of inner mental balance we've been talking about. When this happens, you may be surprised that both answers **and** questions turn out differently!

You may find your logical mind resisting some of the things you'll be doing. It wants to understand, to be told what's happening and why it works. If you explain, it will do everything possible to prove you wrong! Resist the temptation to fall back on logic. Step out and try what I'm about to suggest.

The exercises that follow will help you discover what the synchronous state **feels** like, and show you how to achieve it easily and quickly and use it in a variety of ways. But first, a word of caution. You can't change habits overnight. Change takes time, but not necessarily hard, strenuous effort.

One of the first things you'll discover is that neither these

57

exercises nor your life need to be a constant struggle. After you've practiced for a while, you'll find that things go easier. You'll feel better, calmer, and more confident, and you'll **want** to continue with the exercises.

In chapter 4, I discussed the differences between static and dynamic balance and pointed out that you need both kinds. You want to be calm, yet able to call upon your inner reserves in sudden emergencies. We'll start with static balance.

Beginning Exercises

These exercises will help you to greatly increase your overall awareness, develop more efficient and relaxed concentration, and approach problems differently, in what I call the "discovery mode." You are probably muttering now, "What's he talking about? I'm already aware. I know how to concentrate, and what's this about discovery?" Well, try these tests and see:

1. Set your alarm wristwatch or calculator for three minutes. Sit quietly with your eyes closed and fold your hands in your lap. Now, think only of **one thing**, an imaginary point in the middle of your forehead, equidistant from your eyebrows. Visualize that point in your mind. Think about it, and it alone, for three minutes.

If you're like most of us, you had difficulty shutting out extraneous thoughts and were bothered by a more or less constant flow of images. It would probably have been easier if I'd asked you to think of two or three things at once. We are accustomed to simultaneously watching TV and talking, reading the paper and listening to the radio, and so on. It often seems easier to concentrate on several things than to focus on a single thought. But remember, when you divide your attention, you reduce the amount you can give to any one subject.

2. Here's another, this one very simple. Pay close attention. For the next two minutes do **not** think about yourself, your thoughts, or what you're doing. Not so easy, is it?

3. Now this one's a bit more complicated. Sit as before with your eyes closed. Inhale and exhale slowly slowly three or four times until you are breathing naturally from the lower abdomen. When your breathing stabilizes, begin counting each

exhalation, from one to ten, and then start over. Don't worry if you feel the need to sigh periodically. And if you lose count, simply start over again at one. Each time you reach ten, begin the count anew, counting only the exhalations. Do this for a full three minutes.

Did you lose count? Most people do, often several times in a three-minute period. In fact, it may take weeks before you will be able to do this exercise without losing count at all.

What's the point of all this? Well, most of us are easily distracted and seldom in command of our thoughts. We are easily controlled by subtle unrecognized influences. As you practice the exercises that follow, you will become more sensitive to the nuances of concentration and convinced that it is important to be able to exert absolute control over your thoughts. Remember my mention of *kime,* or focus, in the previous chapter? This is what you're working toward, the ability to direct your attention quickly and easily to a single point while, at the same time, maintaining a larger view. The advantages of this are obvious if you think about it for a moment. Have you ever noticed how nice it is when someone at a party seems to lock in on your every word? They seem to be aware of you and you alone. They are focused. The benefits are even more apparent in conflict situations. By being focused, you are able to concentrate fully on your adversary while still being aware of what is going on around and behind you!

The key to increased focus lies in being able to shift quickly and easily to a different state of resonance, from beta to alpha and theta. The most effective way to achieve this is through what are called meditative forms, similar to the three tests you just took. We'll be discussing two forms, mantric and breath, but first, some essential differences between the two.

In the mantric form, such as Transcendental Meditation (TM), the student receives a nonsense word, a mantra. The meditation consits simply of repeating this word over and over in your mind. Typically, the student is encouraged to meditate twice a day, once in the morning, and again in the evening.

In mantric meditation, alpha waves predominate. You tune out extraneous thoughts, noises, and other outside stimuli; that is, you are unaware of the outer world. If there is a clock ticking in the room, you gradually become unaware of the sound.

Breath meditation is different. In breath meditation, you are aware of external sounds, but in a detached objective way. Sudden noises will be registered, but will not startle you. Your brain wave patterns will show more theta waves once you are well into meditation. If you are in a room with a clock, you will hear the ticks, each successive one as loud as the first. In other words, you will not tune them out.

These differences give you a clue to the ways in which meditation can be used. Mantric meditation is useful in learning about altered states, in developing a sense of deep calm, and for increasing concentration. It helps to develop static balance. Breath meditation on the other hand, encourages dynamic balance.

Mantric Meditation

I suggest that you try mantric meditation for at least a month before moving on to breath meditation. There are two reasons for this. First, many people find that it works well for them and want to continue it. Second, it's an easy introduction to altered states. In the early stages, your ability to recognize what you are experiencing is important. You want to know how it feels.

The first task is to choose a mantra. Some teachers make a big thing out of selecting just the right one. It's interesting to note that one encyclopedia of mantras lists some 700,000 of them. Some advanced teachers feel that the average person can learn to intone correctly no more than fifteen to twenty mantras in an entire lifetime. So, I'm not saying the mantra you choose isn't important, just that unless you're a swami it doesn't make that much difference.

I recommend that beginning students pick one that is simple (one or two syllables), easy to intone, and meaningless, and that feels good when they say it. In teaching, I use the sound, Ahuuuuuum. For most people, it meets the qualifications. If you prefer, you can use Ohmmmmmmm, Immmmmmmmm (as in him), Aaaaaaaa, or even make up your own.

The practice is simple. Sit down in a comfortable chair, fold your hands as before, close your eyes, and begin repeating the mantra silently in your mind. Don't say it with your lips and don't try to control it. Repeat it at whatever speed feels comfortable. If extraneous thoughts intrude, observe them uncritically, allow them to pass, and return to your mantra. Do this for ten minutes at first, then gradually increase your practice period to fifteen or twenty minutes. Aim for two sessions a day, one in the morning and one in the evening. And keep the following guidelines in mind:

Attitude. Don't treat the practice or your mantra lightly. In time, the mantra will become part of your deeper consciousness, develop its own identity, and may even change in form. Do **not** use it to put yourself to sleep (we'll talk about sleep later). And generally, it's a good practice not to discuss your mantra or your meditation with others. If you do, you only invite criticism and needless questions.

Place. Choose a quiet place, free of noise and traffic and preferably with subdued light. Silence the phone and the family (lovingly, please!).

Time. Morning is best, preferably soon after you've gotten up and while the house is quiet. Evening is next best, but not after a full meal or alcohol. Meditation on an empty stomach is infinitely preferable to listening to the digestive juices working, and alcohol inhibits effective mental action. Be attentive to your feelings. You will sense which times are best for you. When you do, set regular times and stick to them. Consistency is especially important in the first few weeks.

Timing. You can peek at your watch from time to time to see if your twenty minutes are up. A better way is to buy a small calculator or watch alarm. They're easy to use and relatively unobtrusive when they sound. In time, you'll develop your own mental alarm clock that will bring you back. You will simply **think** how long you want to meditate, and you'll find yourself coming out quite close to the time you've chosen. Incidently, I make it a practice to do at least one open-ended session a week in which I set no time limits, but just come out when I feel like it, typically, somewhere between forty-five minutes and an hour. These sessions usually involve more than mantric meditation, however, and are better deferred until you have had several months experience.

Distractions. You should be comfortable when you meditate. The exact position is less important than the fact that it allows you to become free of distractions. If you're comfortable sitting with your legs crossed in the lotus position, fine. If not, an upright chair will do. Do not lie down or sit with your head supported, since these positions are more conducive to sleep than meditation.

If you itch, scratch. Too often, a beginner tries to ignore a nagging itch, an uncomfortable position, or a desire to cough. Don't. Attend to the distraction gently and resume your meditation.

Internal distractions are often the more troublesome ones. A continuous flow of random thoughts and images sometimes intrudes. Normally, these will subside after a few minutes. They are best dealt with by simply observing them without judgment, allowing them to pass from awareness, and returning to the meditation. Occasionally, new students are bothered by this mental circus. They shouldn't be. This parade of trivia is often a sign of the mind ridding itself of extraneous thoughts that inhibit concentration. If you can't get rid of the noise, try spending a few sessions simply observing the thoughts as they occur, without any attempt to control or judge them. Often, this will cause them to diminish and allow you to return to your meditation. As noted earlier, occasional thoughts are to be expected.

Coming out. When the alarm rings, come out slowly. Take a full two minutes to open your eyes and come back to the waking state. Allow your eyes to adopt a soft focus; that is, don't look sharply at any given object. Instead, take in all within the range of your vision. Move your hands and arms slowly. Stretch gently. Get up and move about slowly and deliberately for a few minutes. Above all, don't jump up, get in your car, and drive off. You need time to adjust to the waking state again.

Keeping a record. It's a good idea to keep a brief log in the early stages of your meditation experiences. It doesn't have to be fancy or lengthy. A pad of note paper will do. Note the time, date, duration, and anything you experienced that seems significant.

Revelations. Beware of sudden insights during your meditation. They are common for beginning students and seldom important. It takes time and practice to separate the significant from the trivial. Eventually, you will be able to detect the difference. Meanwhile, test every revelation in the cold light of day. If you are puzzled about things that come to you repeatedly, record them in your log so that you can refer to them later.

Continuing problems. A few people find that mantric meditation is not for them. They report great apprehension regarding their sessions, headaches, and other minor physical discomforts. If, after a decent trial, you feel uncomfortable with the mantric form, simply drop it and move on to the breath meditation we'll be discussing later.

It is also natural for new students to find that they require more sleep during the early stages of a meditation program. There is a reason for that. The body stores up tension that is released through meditation. Since tension often masks fatigue, you may feel suddenly tired and need more sleep each night. If so, find a way to get it. After a couple of weeks, you'll probably require less sleep. The relaxing effects of meditation are cumulative. And incidentally, meditation gives you more rest than napping. Some say fifteen minutes of deep meditation is equivalent to an hour of normal sleep.

Now let's assess your progress. You have been meditating for at least a month. During that time, you've left your autobiography and questions pretty much untouched. You are comfortable with your meditation and have noticed changes in your outlook. You feel more calm and are less likely to become irritable. You look forward to your meditation sessions and miss the feeling when you have to skip one. You find that you are less influenced by others and more willing to rely on your own intuition. You discover that you are more curious in a detached playful way, and occasionally, you may catch yourself laughing at something you've said or done. All in all, you take life less seriously.

You may find too, that your views have changed in critical areas. You're less concerned about being "right." You're more willing to turn off the TV or put down the paper than before. And you may find yourself edging away from people at parties who rattle on endlessly about nothing in particular. You sense a new set of priorities in your life, and you aren't concerned that they are less specific than, earlier, you would have liked them to be. You're beginning to develop a new sense of yourself; you're becoming more confident, more willing to risk, and less concerned about the future. And finally, you have the feeling that somebody up there likes you. This isn't necessarily a state of great reverence so much as an inner conviction that you are a significant part of something bigger. You probably can't verbalize these feelings; you shouldn't try. Just go with it and enjoy them. They are all facets of the developing warrior spirit in yourself.

I'm telling you this because many of these results may seem strange at first. We'll be talking more about this in chapter 7, so don't worry if it doesn't make complete sense now. Just continue with the exercises and enjoy the experience.

Before we go on to the breath form, I want to discuss two very practical applications of meditation: problem solving and sleep induction.

Problem Solving

Most of us are accustomed to struggling with problems and are upset when solutions aren't immediately apparent. By now, you've probably sensed there's another way. To begin with, you may have already experienced the sensation of having problems solve themselves. You may have been conscious of a problem but have done nothing to solve it, when suddenly the solution just popped out at you. While this is useful when it happens spontaneously, there is a way you can encourage it. In fact, you can apply the technique to some of the questions and issues that emerged from your autobiography.

First, get ready; have a pencil and pad nearby. Sit quietly for a few moments and get a feeling for the problem you're trying to solve. Don't analyze it or try to state it precisely. Just get the sense of it, and then begin counting your breaths as before, from one to ten. Do this for three or four complete ten-count cycles. When you feel very calm, begin another count, only this time count differently. Imagine that you are at the top of a flight of stairs or at the crest of a hill. Begin walking downward and, as you do, count each step. There are ten steps in all. With each one, you feel more relaxed, quiet, and peaceful. By the fifth step, your body begins to feel very light. By the seventh, you are virtually unaware of your body at all. When you reach ten, you seem to be floating rather than walking.

Now, don't reach for it, just allow the problem to enter your consciousness. Let it drift into view as a picture or a feeling. What does it feel or look like? Does it have a particular form? Look gently at it. Get a sense of the total problem. As you look, ask yourself if there is anything unusual about the picture (or the feeling). Wait a few moments for an answer. Then look more closely. Does the problem have obvious parts? What are they? Again, don't analyze; just observe. Do the parts look different from what you thought they might?

Somewhere in this process of gentle questioning, you may experience a sudden feeling that you've got hold of something, that something has changed, perhaps that the solution is right at your fingertips. This feeling is often accompanied by a physical response as well—a dropping of the shoulders, a sigh, or a sense of being even more relaxed. The specifics vary, but they all involve some bodily reaction that is unexpected, but not unpleasant. When this happens, note it and ask yourself: "What do I sense about this problem that is new?" Wait for an answer, but don't be impatient or expectant. Just wait. Sit quietly for a minute or two and simply observe what is happening. When you feel you have a clear sense of the picture, turn and begin walking up the hill or the stairs. Count yourself up in reverse order . . . 10, 9, 8, and so on. When you reach the top, open your eyes slowly. Come out just as you would from any meditation. Sit quietly and review what you have observed. Does the problem appear different now? Take a moment to jot down any ideas that have come to you. Don't worry about organizing them. Just put them down as they occur so that you can refer back to them later.

This kind of problem solving takes practice. The more you use it, the better it works. Don't expect dramatic results the first few times. You are tapping into areas of consciousness and energy that you don't normally use. Call it the collective unconscious, divine guidance, whatever. Don't try to pinpoint its source at this point.

Getting to Sleep

Many people have trouble sleeping. They go to sleep with their problems and wake up more tired than when they went to bed. If this sounds familiar, you'll be happy to know that you don't need to put up with such harassment. You can simply turn off the light, put yourself to sleep in a few minutes, and wake up thoroughly refreshed. How?

Simply use a modified version of the counting method you've just learned. Lie down and get into a comfortable position. I find that lying on my back with my legs and arms parallel provides the best body alignment. If you are comfortable with that position, it's a good place to start. Now when you're set, take a deep breath, hold it for a few seconds, and then slowly exhale from the lower abdomen. Repeat this two or three times and be sure that your exhalations are long and steady. Now breathe normally in long, even breaths. If you have a tendency to yawn, go ahead, then return to your breathing. Again, concentrate on exhaling rather than inhaling. Allow your body to settle deeper into the bed with each exhalation.

Mentally check your body to see if you are relaxed. Begin at your toes and continue with each bodily part—feet, ankles, legs, thighs, back, stomach, and so on, one by one. If you sense that a particular muscle is tight, focus your attention on it and tell it to relax. If it is still tight, tense it as hard as you can for about ten seconds and then relax. Follow this process for your whole body, including your face and scalp. When you've finished, focus on your breathing again. Allow it to become gentle, effortless, and regular. By now you should be breathing almost entirely in the lower abdomen. Begin your count as before, only this time don't stop at ten. Go on to twenty or even thirty if you need to. With a little practice, you'll find that you seldom reach twenty, and sometimes you won't even reach ten.

I've taught this technique to many people, and it works. One woman's husband snored like a locomotive. She learned to put herself to sleep even with him snoring in the bed next to her. If his snoring woke her up in the middle of the night, she would apply the technique again to get back to sleep.

Sleep and Problem Solving

You may experience what I call spontaneous problem solving. It most often occurs when you've been worrying about a problem and have used the sleep-induction method to get to sleep. In the morning, you wake up with a solution! You have applied the problem-solving approach in your sleep without being aware of it.

This happened to me during a period of great personal stress. I was working on several problems that refused to yield and found it difficult to get to sleep. On several mornings, while only semiconscious, answers appeared as pictures in my mind like scenes from a slide projector. I was later able to verify their accuracy. They were correct in every detail!

Before I began following the practices I'm describing, nothing of this sort ever happened to me. Once begun, however, it was like pulling the stopper in a bathtub. I began to "see," differently. Once, in a complicated business negotiation, I found myself unaccountably violating a strategy agreed upon with our lawyers and accountants, and it worked. On other occasions, I began to sense others' feelings and thoughts as though they were my own. At first, it was difficult to distinguish between my thoughts and theirs. Gradually, things sorted themselves out. As I learned to put myself into a waking altered state, these abilities increased. Clarity and certainty are a function of time and practice. You can't rush the process, but it does happen if you are patient and attentive.

These examples will give you some idea of the many applications of altered states. Meditation provides a foundation of deep calm, relaxed concentration, and unusual clarity. It's a way of tuning in to your deeper powers. Your meditation will have both immediate and long-range effects. Each session will recharge, revitalize, and rebalance. Over time, the cumulative effects of meditation help you to shift away from the reactive mode.

Breath Meditation

Up to now, your practice has been confined to mantric meditation, which, as I pointed out, is most useful in developing static balance and calm. Now we're going to take a look at breath meditation, specifically a variant of the form used in Zen training. We will be discussing five different types of breath meditation, which will be presented pretty much in the order you'll want to try them. I might add, these five can keep you busy for a lifetime. But before we get into the specific forms, there are several points to note about breathing.

Many of us are "reverse breathers" much of the time, that is, we breathe primarily in our chests. Reverse breathing is both a cause and an effect of stress. It is nearly impossible to be relaxed if you are chest breathing; it simply takes too much effort. Notice someone under severe stress, especially if they're sobbing and note how their chest heaves as they breathe. Chest breathing is abnormal breathing, despite the fact that many of us do it.

There is another reason why chest breathing is bad. Our lungs have a maximum capacity of about 5,700 milliliters. In normal respiration, we breathe in an extremely narrow range, say between 2,300 and 2,800 milliliters. Through correct abdominal breathing, the volume of air actually exchanged can be increased dramatically, by as much as 1,100 milliliters, thus supplying the body with a continually greater flow of oxygen. The significance of this increased flow becomes more apparent when you remember that the brain consumes about a fourth of all of the oxygen utilized in the body. Efficient breathing, therefore, can greatly improve the effectiveness of mental functions.

Initial breathing difficulties. Beginning meditators often have problems stabilizing their breathing. Feelings that the pattern is forced, a feeling of mild claustrophobia, and a need to sigh frequently are common. With practice, those sensations will pass. The more you practice, the more effortless your breathing will become.

Exhalation. We all tend to be more concerned with getting air into the lungs than expelling it. When you think about it, that doesn't make sense. Nature abhors a vacuum, in the world and in the lungs. If you succeed in emptying your lungs of air, nature will fill them automatically. Yet in athletics, health classes, and even in some music instruction, we are taught to take deep chest-filling breaths.

Concentrate instead on exhaling. Allow the air to come into your lungs and then gently expel it from them. Your exhalation should be long and smooth, beginning in the lower abdomen and flowing from the mouth in a controlled manner. At first, you may find yourself exhaling (and counting) in pushes. You may even find that you breathe and count in time with your pulse. Don't worry. As you become more comfortable with the process, your exhalations will become natural and effortless.

When you meditate using the breath, think only of exhaling from the lower abdomen or *hara*. You'll know if you are breathing properly because abdominal breathing results in a noticeably lower sound than chest breathing. Ultimately, you'll not be concerned with inhaling or exhaling, and will do both in a balanced relaxed way. But for now, concentrate on exhaling.

The inhalation-exhalation transition. You should make the transition from inhalation to exhalation smoothly and without a pause. At first this will require a conscious effort. With practice, however, the transition can be made almost without noticing it. Conversely, at the end of the exhalation phase, you may find it useful to pause briefly and feel the particular calm that attends that point in the cycle. The pause should not be forced, but should occur naturally as a moment of waiting. Some teachers of meditation contend that great insights come in these brief pauses.

Position of the head. You can best discover how to hold your head by experiment. Ideally, you want the head tilted slightly forward so as to allow an unrestricted flow of air to the lungs when your eyes are cast downward at a point two or three feet in front of you. Move your head as far forward as you can and then all the way back. Those are the outer limits that define the range within which you can move.

Now let's explore each of the five forms of breath meditation. Remember, they are all variations of *zazen*, the form taught in Zen and used widely in the martial arts. Zen is the philosophical underpinning of many of the martial arts and, to many, a welcome change from the excessive intellectuality of western religion and philosophy. It is not the purpose of this book to present a course in either Zen or the martial arts but to convey the universal aspects of both. If you are interested in Zen as a formal discipline, there are many texts and a growing number of Zen societies available.

The Ten Count. This is the same form you practiced earlier as a self-test, so we won't dwell on it now. It consists simply of counting your exhalations repeatedly, from one to ten. This is an exercise in precise concentration, which contributes directly to the dynamic balance we talked about earlier. In breath meditation, you'll recall, you don't tune out your surroundings but are aware of them in a detached way. You are dynamically balanced.

We've talked about posture in connection with mantric meditation. Your posture is especially important in breath meditation, because it directly effects the flow of oxygen to the lower abdomen. Improper posture will interfere with effective concentration. You can be assured of having good posture if you follow these guidelines:

1. Sit with your knees lower than your buttocks. You can adopt the lotus position (or any variation of it) or the *seiza* position, in which you kneel, sit on your lower legs, and cross the large toes of each foot (right over left), or you can sit in a chair if you prefer. Whichever position you adopt, stay with it throughout the meditation.

2. Sit belly forward, buttocks back so that your spine is straight when viewed from the front, but curved forward at the lumbar region when viewed from the side. This encourages smooth air flow and effective concentration.

3. Now lower the chest and shoulders. Don't force them down, just allow them to relax.

Following the above guidelines will enable you to relax the upper body and place minimal tension of the region of the lower abdomen. Experimentation is the best way of finding the correct posture. Stick with the ten-count form until you can routinely complete a dozen or more cycles flawlessly. By then you will have vastly increased your concentrative power and discovered how much it can do for you.

Breath Following. This is an extremely simple form, one that will be more meaningful when you have a solid grounding in the ten-count method. It consists simply in becoming aware only of your breaths, in and out. You observe your breathing, but make no effort to control it. This is an interim form that joins the ten-count and one-point methods. It will help you become more calm and gain greater detachment.

One phenomenon that frequently occurs during meditation is called *makyo* in Japanese. *Makyo* are visions, hallucinations, or especially vivid perceptions of color or sound. If you encounter them, my advice is the same as that given by all Zen teachers: Ignore them! They are rarely significant. If you dwell on them, they will inhibit your progress.

One-point Breath Meditation. When you have mastered the ten-count and breath-following forms, move on to this one. It is a combination of mantric and breath meditation. It will help reinforce the centering exercises presented in the previous chapter.

One-point breath meditation is performed as follows: Breathe as before and, as you exhale, mentally focus on your one point or *hara*. Initially, you may want to mentally intone the word "one." In time, however, you will learn to simply visualize the one point. You can start by visualizing a ball that you gradually shrink in size until it becomes a single point.

Again what's the **point** of this? What is the one point? Well, in its most basic form, it's a focus for your meditation. But it is also **your** center, your *hara*, the place where everything balances. As you progress further, you will see that it's not a physical place. It is **you**, the absolute center of you and the universe, the ultimate coincidence of mind and human being, the place from which all power emanates. It is the core of the warrior spirit.

Power Meditation. You may want to try this form occasionally when you feel mentally fatigued or emotionally drained. It consists simply of visualizing power flowing inwardly *to* the one point as you inhale, and then outwardly *from* the one point as you exhale. Begin your meditation with either the ten count or the one point, and then gently begin visualizing the flow of power through the nostrils, passing through and cleansing the brain, the spinal cord, the heart, on down into the lower abdomen. You may find it helpful to visualize colors, beginning with light pink and moving to lavender, blue, green, yellow, red, and white. Notice how different colors affect the meditation. For example, does red fill you with high energy? How do you feel when you visualize blue? White?

Absolute Stillness. The Japanese term for this form is *shikan-taza*. It means mindlessness and consists of sitting quietly and doing nothing. By now, you know this isn't as easy as it seems. We're always doing something even if it's only thinking.

If you've stayed with me till now, you can understand why I didn't discuss this form earlier. For many people, sitting quietly without conscious thought is an impossibility. In fact, it's difficult for anyone and is usually achieved only after many years of practice.

Why do it? What does it do for you? Well, without copping out, I'll say that any attempt to describe its benefits is doomed to failure from the outset. It must be experienced rather than discussed. It is a state of perfect comprehension. It is beyond words, beyond thoughts, and even beyond images. It is, to use a Zen expression, "direct knowing." It is beyond process.

What does it feel like? Well, remember when I asked you to hold your breath for ten seconds and you discovered that you had no conscious thoughts during that period? *Shikan-taza* is a similar state, carried on for a much longer period. No, you don't hold your breath for several minutes! The effect, however, is much the same. When you first began, you may find it extremely tiring. It's a bit like being suspended over a precipice and not wanting to move a muscle for fear you will fall. With practice, **much** practice, you will be able to achieve this state more easily and for longer periods of time. At first, a few seconds may be your maximum. Gradually, however, you can learn to remain free of conscious thoughts for several minutes, and you will discover that this mindlessness is a deeply relaxing and mentally cleansing experience. You will not only be able to control your conscious thought more easily, you will be less likely to accumulate unwanted thoughts.

72

*   *   *

If you've practiced any of these forms for even a month, you have an idea what meditation can do for you. Increased awareness and greater concentration are obvious benefits. But what of the longer term, the subtle shift in attitudes I mentioned? You'll recall that I suggested that meditation would enable you to approach your problems differently, that is, from a basis of spontaneous discovery.

The chapter entitled "The Constructed Self" described the limitations forced upon us by our experience and identified some of the reactive patterns of the logical mind. Meditation helps break those patterns. It is not so much illogical as beyond logic. It leads to a state of balance where intuition and reason cooperate rather than compete.

Reason, logic, and argument have been given preferential positions in our society. We require a radical approach to get us out of these old ruts. Of course you may be jolted out of them by a sudden crisis or a watershed experience. Sudden unexpected highs can provoke new ways of knowing. The problem is, crises and peak experiences are unpredictable. You may wait fifty years for lightning to strike. Moreover, there is growing evidence that these spontaneous rebirths are really the result of long preparation. Students of the creative process have concluded that sudden discoveries are often preceded by long periods of sustained effort. Things happen when we're ready, not before.

Meditation and waking experience are both part of life. Meditative techniques enable you to become more sensitive to new and sometimes illogical information. But neither meditation nor life can be learned in one short course. Both require constant practice.

So far, we've been talking about mental development. We're going to shift gears rapidly in the next chapter and talk about fitness and how it relates to the discovery process. We won't be talking about sports fitness or about becoming a martial artist, a marathoner, or a weight lifter. We will be concerned with the intricate and subtle relationships that exist between mind and body, and how they can help you discover more about yourself and your world.

You may already have an exercise program that works well for you. If so, I urge that you stick with it. Read the next chapter and incorporate the exercises and principles that seem useful. But remember, **physical** fitness is only one reason for exercising. A much more important purpose of regular rigorous exercise is that it enables you to engage in a meaningful dialogue with your body. In becoming fit, you gain confidence in the body's ability and you trust the messages it sends. So, while physical well-being is essential, it's the psychic benefit that flows from an acknowledged partnership between mind and body that concerns us most. Your body is both a receiver and a transmitter, which you can tune to an incredible level of sensitivity. This is what lifelong fitness is all about.

CHAPTER SIX
TUNING THE BODY

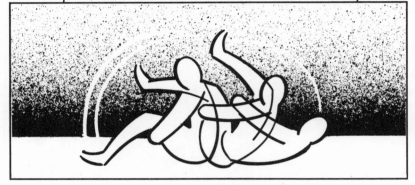

L ou and John were classmates but not friends. Lou was loud, confident, aggressive, 240 pounds, and the school's boxing champion, first-string tackle, and starting first baseman. As the youngest of three brothers, he learned to fight almost as soon as he could walk.

John was quiet, slender, studious and except for tennis which he played poorly, avoided athletics. Often, he slept until noon and worked past midnight, poring over physics and math assignments.

Now, thirty years later, Lou is dead at forty-seven. He died of a heart attack, thirty pounds overweight, a heavy smoker, an avid football fan, and a business success. John is alive, thin as ever, and still quiet except when he talks about running. He began about ten years ago in an effort to rebuild his relationship with his teenage son, which had been going downhill. On advice from a friend, John picked up the only common thread he could find. The boy liked to run, had joined the school track and cross-country teams, and chided his father for being out of shape. John maintains that running his changed his life. He says it taught him about himself and about his connection with others, especially with his son. I asked him why he runs marathons, a practice he took up two years ago. "I guess because they take me to places I've never been before, in my head, I mean," he replied. "They give me a sense of aliveness I've never known. And no matter how many I run, it's nice to know there's always one more."

Lou, the athlete, is dead. John, the nonathlete who regards running as a way of life, is alive. Why? Why did Lou succumb to the arm chair and the weekend sports spectaculars? And why has John chosen to force himself to the extremes of athletic endeavor?

Until quite recently, boys' coaches emphasized sports for all of the wrong reasons—to build character, to become more competitive, and to win. Whose character? To win what? For many coaches, character and ego are one, and competition means winning at any cost. Their methods bear an eerie resemblance to Marine boot camp—pressure, threats, abuse, humiliation, and drugstore philosophy. In their attempts to turn boys into men, they drive many away from sports altogether and cause others to lose their enthusiasm as soon as there are no more ribbons, trophies, or letters.

Our culture reinforces this alienation. We're encouraged to overeat and underexercise, to pickle and burn our bodies, and then correct it all with diet and pills. We are seldom told what our bodies **can** do, only what they must be **made** to do.

In reality, body and mind are a team, two giant computers capable of working in close harmony. The slightest movement of mind is mirrored instantly on the body, and every bodily event is transmitted to the mind just as quickly. This interlocking circuitry is nothing short of amazing. It is also a major source of conflict. If either one suffers a system malfunction, receives conflicting data, or is instructed incorrectly, the other instantly knows, reacts, and attempts to right the situation. Soon they are at war, each pulling in a different direction, neither willing to give an inch, and both caught up in a common dilemma. The key to unscrambling the mess lies in the relationship between the two. Both must be equally prepared, similarly informed, and singularly directed. We must rediscover the original harmony and rebuild the partnership.

Body As System

The body is like a car. It requires continuous maintenance and periodic tuning to make it run well. It thrives on performance. A well-tuned body is more like a Porsche Turbo than a Volkswagen Bug. Racing down the autobahn, the VW strains to reach top speed, to catch up and keep up, and uses every ounce of its power. The Porsche, on the other hand, cruises at partial power, accelerates smoothly, and passes easily, still well below peak performance. Properly maintained, body and Porsche are marvelous machines.

Unfortunately for most of us, our bodies are not tuned for maximum performance. We perform well below our potential in almost all areas. Our senses of hearing, taste, smell, touch, and sight are dulled by our own technology. Additives, noise, pollution, and maltreatment make us shadows of ourselves. We no longer trust the body's messages, because we've screwed up the transmitter and mistuned the receiver. The horrible result is not that we don't get any signals but that we get the wrong ones and misinterpret them. We suffer diseases of inactivity and do even less. We eat our way to one extreme, starve the body to the very things it needs to repair itself, and then substitute chemical concoctions that we aren't sure will work. It is testimony to the remarkable nature of the human body that it works as long as it does.

How can you get in touch with the body again, patch up old wounds, and rebuild a sense of mutual trust? When you've repeatedly slandered an old friend, robbed him of his dignity and destroyed his faith, rebuilding takes time. But there are things you can do. You can begin by understanding what the body and fitness are all about.

Both cars and bodies are made up of systems, all of which must be fit for optimum functioning. The body has at least ten:

- **Muscular,** the skeletal muscles, which help move the frame about
- **Circulatory,** the heart, blood, and blood vessels, which deliver nutrients and oxygen and transport wastes
- **Digestive,** the mouth, stomach, and intestines, which process and absorb foods and liquids and dispose of waste products
- **Urinary,** the kidneys, bladder, and related organs, which rid the body of wastes and control blood makeup
- **Reproductive,** the genitals and all those other good things that keep the race growing
- **Nervous,** the brain and spinal cord, which, as you learned earlier, affect awareness and control many bodily functions

- **Endocrine,** hormonal glands such as the thyroid and the pituitary, which control metabolism and growth
- **Lymphatic,** the tonsils, spleen, and nodes, which form blood cells, replace bodily tissue, and help maintain immunity from disease
- **Integumentary,** the skin, hair, nails, and skin glands, which provide temperature control and protection and contribute to your good looks.

Most of the time these systems operate pretty much automatically. It's only when they malfunction or are mistreated that the mind is called in to help. At those critical times we sense the relationship between mind and body is closer than we think. The more we discover about these hidden relationships, the more we find out there is to know.

Fitness As Awareness

The right amounts and kinds of food and exercise coupled with healthful living habits can do wonders to tune the human machine, keep the systems fit, and prepare for peak performance. Fitness is not just being free from disease; it is positive health, effective physical and mental functioning over one's entire lifespan. But it is even more. Fitness is heightened awareness, the extraordinary sensitivity of mind and body that makes all life an adventure and renders you happier, more complete, and more dedicated to learning, growing, and discovering. The fit person is one whose body and mind are honed to razor sharpness and who delights in the use of both.

There are lots of ways of keeping fit—running, skiing, weight lifting, tennis, handball—and we'll be discussing them within the context of aerobic and anerobic exercises. But before we do, let's consider two basic aspects of becoming fit: breathing and flexibility.

Breath is power. We've discussed breath as a meditative form and as a bridge between static and dynamic balance. Just as correct meditative breathing can increase your mental power, so correct breathing while exercising can heighten your physical power. If you don't believe me, try a simple experiment. Pick out a heavy object such as a basket of wet laundry or a concrete block, something you have to bend over to lift. First, lift it by inhaling and holding your breath. Note how heavy it feels. Now lift it again, only this time exhale as you lift. Do you notice how much lighter it feels?

You've probably been taught the importance of deep breathing by your high-school coach or P.E. instructor. In all probability, he or she emphasized deep **inhalation.** From your meditation, you know that **exhalation** is the more important of the two. Remember, the lungs will fill automatically, but emptying them requires action on your part. Correct breathing is abdominal breathing, coupled with an awareness of the importance of correct exhalation. The next time you're winded from strenuous exertion, take a moment and forcefully expel the air from your lungs in three or four loud bursts. Make a loud sound, Aaaaaaah, each time. Note how quickly you recover! I've taught this technique to people who have moved to Denver (5,280 feet high) from sea level and have trouble with dizziness. They invariably find that the dizziness vanishes once they learn to exhale as they stand up.

Poor breathing habits are not changed overnight. Constant practice is required until correct breathing patterns are firmly established. You can practice anytime, while sitting, walking, jogging, or driving. It's a matter of deciding to do it. Let's assume you're in your car. Take a moment to get relaxed, positioned squarely in your seat with your upper body in a comfortably erect position. Now inhale just as you did in the initial stages of breath meditation. As you reach the maximum volume with which you are comfortable, hold your breath for a couple of seconds. Allow the air to settle into the lower abdomen. Now exhale in a steady, firm manner through your mouth. If there's no one else in the car, make a low Aaaaaaaah sound as you exhale. It should take you about twice as long to exhale as to inhale. When you've expelled the air from your lungs, pause a couple of seconds before inhaling. Note how calm you feel. Learn to experience this calm at the end of each exhalation. The entire cycle should take about forty-five seconds. Trained martial artists can extend the cycle to a full minute or more. Oh yes, if you're doing this exercise while driving, **keep your** eyes open! It is so relaxing that you can easily drift into an altered state. Approximately twenty minutes are required to exchange all of the air in the body. When you've finished, you will feel relaxed and invigorated even down to your toes and fingertips. In the martial arts, this is known as "breath cleansing" and is regarded as having therapeutic benefits in combating illness. If you practice regularly, you'll find your breathing patterns will gradually stabilize and become more efficient.

Flexibility is mental. To many people, flexibility means bouncing, bobbing, and contorting the body to make it more supple. Recall the coach who shouted at you, "Stretch those hamstrings!" That kind of stretching only shortens the muscles and can cause serious injuries. In fact, most exercise shortens the muscles. When a muscle is forced to extend, it invariably reacts by contracting. If you jog, take a moment before starting out, sit on the floor with your legs stretched out in front and note how far you can bend forward. Then after your run, try it again. Notice the difference.

Flexibility enables you to do more with less effort and less risk of injury. It is a function of practice. One of the big differences between beginning and advanced karate students is that beginning students are invariably tight and awkward in their movements, whereas advanced students move with a smooth, easy fluidity. Remember the centering exercises from chapter 4 and the lesson you learned from them: to be centered and extend power, you must be relaxed. The more flexible you are, the easier it is to relax.

I'm going to give you a set of eleven movements to increase your flexibility. Once you master them, they can be completed in about five minutes. These are **physical** movements, but they can have profound **mental** benefits if you do them correctly. For each one, visualize the flow of power just as you did in the centering exercises. **Feel** your muscles lengthening and your entire body becoming a channel for the flow of energy. Breathe abdominally and think of **allowing** your muscles, tendons, and ligaments to relax and become flexible. Every movement should feel good! You are allowing the body to relax and extend, not **forcing** it. Here are the eleven:

1. Sit on a carpeted floor, knees drawn up so that your heels are about a foot from your buttocks. Reach around your thighs and grasp one wrist with the opposite hand. Your arms are now clasped underneath the crook framed by your legs. Gently allow yourself to roll back on your shoulders, exhaling as you roll. Do this four or five times making sure that you are as relaxed as possible throughout your entire body. You will frequently note a popping in the spinal vertabrae. Good! This is a sign of relaxation, a loosening of the spinal column. With practice, you'll be able to adjust the vertabrae effortlessly and you'll enjoy the relaxation it affords.

2. Sit, this time with your legs extended and your feet together. Fold your arms over your chest and lean forward, exhaling at the same time. Don't force it. Just allow the weight of your arms, head, and shoulders to gently extend the muscles of the lower back and legs. Relax completely. Feel the muscles gradually lengthening. Hold this position for about a minute.

3. Now, still sitting, gently draw one leg up and place the sole of your foot against the opposite knee, allowing both legs to remain completely relaxed. Reach forward and grasp your calf, ankle, or foot, whichever you can do comfortably. Lean forward, exhale, and relax. Feel the gentle pressure on the

extended leg. Hold this position for about thirty seconds while breathing normally, then do it for the other side as well.

4. While sitting on the floor, spread your legs as wide as you can comfortably. Now lean toward either leg, exhaling in the process. You may want to grasp your calf or ankle with the respective hand (right hand to right calf). As you lean, position your body so that the shoulder of the holding hand is aimed toward that leg, and let your other hand, now over your head, point toward that foot. Depending on the position of the raised arm, you will feel a pull on the lateral muscles running from waist to armpit. Hold this position for ten to fifteen seconds, and then switch to the other side.

5. Still in a seated position, lean toward the floor to a point midway between your outstretched legs, exhaling gradually as you lean. Do this with your arms folded and let the weight of your arms, head, and shoulders lower your upper body. Hold this position for about forty-five seconds as you breathe naturally. Feel your body relaxing, and note the gradual extension of your inner thigh muscles.

6. Now sit sprinter's style, one leg tucked under the buttocks. Draw the leg up only as far as you're comfortable. Rotate your body at the waist toward the tucked leg, supporting yourself with your hands if necessary. This motion tends to stretch the upper thigh muscles (quadriceps) in the tucked leg. Do this three or four times on each side.

7. Stand and gently clasp your hands behind you while bending forward and exhaling. Feel the pull on your shoulders. Concentrate on your shoulder blades. Let all of your muscles relax as the pressure on your shoulder blades gradually increases. Stretch gently, much as you would after awaking from a nap.

8. Now let your arms hang at your sides. Slowly swing your arms, first to the right and then to the left. Allow your arms to flop back and forth. Let everything hang loose. While

they are swinging, keep your eyes and shoulders facing forward. Focus gently on some distant point. Do this for fifteen or twenty seconds.

9. Stand quietly and rotate your neck in a circle and in a combination of forward, back, left, and right. Make gentle movements so that your head seems to float on your shoulders. Continue until your neck feels completely relaxed.

10. Still standing, shake both hands, slowly at first and then more rapidly and vigorously. Shake them until your fingers and wrists are completely relaxed and you feel a tingling sensation in your hands. If you shake hard enough, you'll feel your toes lifting from the floor. Do this for thirty seconds and then gradually slow down until you are standing relaxed and motionless.

11. Stand in front of a mirror, preferably full length. Observe yourself calmly. Look into your eyes. Don't worry about how your hair looks or whether you're skinny or fat. Just observe how calm you are. Resolve to carry this feeling with you throughout the day. Look into your eyes and say, "I will remain calm and relaxed."

You might find it useful, at odd moments during the day, to take a few seconds and shake your hands as described above.

You'll be surprised how quickly this restores your calm. If this seems strange to you, think about what you are doing throughout these exercises. You are creating a relaxed attitude in the body as well as in the mind. You are **allowing** yourself to be more flexible, physically and mentally, and you are becoming centered as well.

Aerobic Fitness

I've talked about the importance of breathing in connection with both meditation and exercise, and I noted how important oxygen is to the brain. When the body is geared to process oxygen effectively, we say that a person is aerobically fit. That means that the bodily systems can carry oxygen to all parts of the body quickly, easily, and continuously. Aerobic exercise fosters this effectiveness. It consists of physical activities performed with sufficient intensity and duration to significantly raise and maintain pulse and respiratory rates.

Everyone has a maximum heart rate. As a rule of thumb, your maximum rate is found by subtracting your current age from 220. If you are forty years old, your maximum is 180. You can see that this rate declines slowly with age.

In aerobic exercise, you're not trying to achieve your maximum rate. You are aiming at a **training** rate, which is roughly 80 percent of your maximum rate. In the example above, your training rate would be 144. The training rate is really a range rather than a single number. This reflects the fact that there are differences among people. When trained athletes and untrained people perform identical tasks, the athletes do the tasks with relatively lower heart rates.

What we're talking about here is cardiovascular fitness, the ability of the respiratory and circulatory systems to process oxygen. This involves other systems as well. The lungs, for example, have no muscles of their own. They function because of the smooth muscles of the rib cage. Furthermore, the effectiveness of blood as a delivery system depends on the successful operation of the urinary system. So for cardiovascular fitness, all systems must function properly.

Aerobic fitness is important for another reason. It strengthens the heart and increases the size of the blood vessels, thus enabling the heart to pump more blood with fewer strokes. Comparing an athlete to an untrained person, an athlete's heart beats slower, perhaps 10,000 strokes per night less than a normal person. This is another proof that the conditioned individual can do more than less effort. Generally speaking, an athlete's pulse will be fifteen to twenty beats per minute lower than the poorly conditioned individual.

How can you increase your aerobic capacity? What does it take to be aerobically fit? Well, there are lots of ways to do it, and they all have this in common: an elevated heart rate for a prolonged period of time, specifically, up to your training rate for a minimum of twelve minutes. You can walk, run, swim, play tennis or handball, ride a bike, or skip rope. The particular activity you choose is less important than the way you do it. You must pursue it with sufficient intensity to bring your pulse up to the training rate and keep it there. The nice thing about aerobic training is that there are so many ways to do it, all of which allow you to progress gradually and gently. You don't need to be an athlete to become fit. You can start by walking, add some short jogging intervals, and move up to a full-blown running program if you prefer.

You can design your own program or, if you like, simply enter into any one of the many aerobic exercise programs available throughout the country. Before starting on your own, I suggest reading, *The Aerobics Way*.[1] The author, Dr. Kenneth Cooper, runs a sports clinic and research center in Dallas, Texas. Since the center's inception in 1971, Cooper has put thousands of men and women through evaluation and training programs. Cooper has also coauthored, with his wife, Mildred, another book, *Aerobics for Women*.[2] Both are excellent sources. They contain tables for self-evaluation, guidelines, and graduated aerobic programs in a dozen or more activities, from running to bicycling.

Cooper has devised a point system in which you build gradually to thirty points a week (twenty-four for women). You gain points in different ways, such as:

[1] Kenneth H. Cooper, M.D., M.P.H., *The Aerobics Way*
[2] Mildred Cooper and Kenneth Cooper, *Aerobics for Women*

- Walking three miles, four times a week, in forty-three minutes or less for each walk
- Running two miles, four times a week, in twenty-one minutes or less
- Swimming 800 yards, four times a week, in sixteen minutes or less each time
- Skipping rope five times a week (90–100 steps/minute) for fifteen minutes each time

Aerobic exercise affects all of the body's systems. It is absolutely essential for total fitness, and contributes to the mental/physical links between breath and awareness. As you breathe properly and exercise aerobically, you will observe a rekindling of the partnership between mind and body. Each supports the other.

Let's talk about running, for a moment. Running is the most popular aerobic activity today, but many people still regard it as a bloody bore. You don't have to be a runner to run. You have only to enjoy walking. Let me say it another way. You start where you are. Many who have discovered running late in life have found that it is an excellent way to learn about yourself, a time to be alone with your thoughts and your body, and an activity in which you can definitely **win.** You win because you are not competing with your body; you are learning what it can do for you. This learning can be richly rewarding, as is eloquently attested to by Dr. George Sheehan in his book, *This Running Life.*[3] Dr. Sheehan, now past sixty, ran in his youth, dropped it for years, and then began again at age fifty. He resumed running purely for exercise and has become an accomplished marathoner. Dr. Sheehan writes with simple beauty about the joys of running and about the inner life available to all of us. As a friend of mine remarked, "George could make a turtle want to run!"

As a runner you choose your own time, place, and distance. You seek or avoid companions and pick your own scenery, run fast or slow, long or short, hot or cold, all according to your own choosing. If you see a flower or bird that interests you, you

[3]George A. Sheehan, M.D., *This Running Life*

stop to look and listen until your body tells you it's time to move on. You rediscover, in those few minutes each day, the indescribable joy of being part of the wind, sun, and sky. You follow a physical path to a mental goal. You find that running is meditation, a vacation from problems, worries, and boredom.

You feel superior to those who only walk or sit. Not only is your pulse slower and your blood pressure more normal, you have more energy and use less of it than your unconditioned colleague. You rest quickly and easily and work hard as well. You sit down at the table with less appetite and get up knowing that your systems are performing efficiently. As one of my friends observed, "Constipation is unknown to the long-distance runner." That's true. The runner's body is geared to a higher production of naturally laxative magnesium. He or she is a finely tuned machine!

But how much is enough? How often do you need to run or play tennis? I exercise five or six times a week—twenty to thirty miles running (at 8,000 feet), two weight workouts, and assorted martial-arts form practices. I do much more than is required to remain fit. For most people, I recommend three aerobic workouts a week, thirty minutes each, and two weight or calisthenics workouts. Yes, that's a lot, but remember, you can trade in your car, but not your body.

Muscular Fitness

As you get older, the argument for bulging biceps becomes less appropriate, if it ever was. A doctor friend was stationed in Korea during the war. He took tissue samples of men killed in action and found that tissue from heavily muscled bodies was rippled with fat, much like choice beefsteak! For most of us, the last thing we need is more fat. It is questionable whether that extra bulk is either necessary or healthful over the long run.

There is, however, an excellent case to be made for muscular fitness. Most aerobic programs do not provide adequate muscle development. Runners, for example, are weak in quadricep, abdominal, and upper-body muscles. Weight-training programs, on the other hand, are generally anaerobic, that is, they do not increase the heart rate long enough to produce sufficient aerobic training effect. Both aerobic and muscular fitness are needed.

Should you work with weights or without? Should your routine be isotonic or isometric? Should your muscle workout be once, twice, or three times a week? How long should you exercise at a time? What principles govern muscle development? Let's take each of these in turn.

Whether you use weights or not is a matter of personal choice. If you travel a lot, a weight routine may be impractical. On the other hand, weights have several advantages over calisthenics. They allow greater precision in terms of how much and what you exercise. They offer easy tradeoffs between endurance and strength. Higher repetitions with lower weights build tone and endurance. Lower repetitions with higher weights build bulk and power. And weight training accomplishes more in less time than calisthenics.

Calisthenics. Let's assume for a moment that weights are out of the question, that you want a simple and quick routine you can do in a hotel room (on the days you're not running!). Here's what I recommend:

1. *Warmup.* Repeat your morning flexibility routine and add to it some easy jumping jacks or light running in place, anything to increase your heart rate and cause you to begin perspiring. (Skip flexibility step 11, mirror-gazing).

2. *Half-squats.* Grasp a doorknob or the edge of a table in both hands. Lower your body as though you were seated in a chair with your back straight. Now alternately raise and lower your body while keeping your back straight. Begin with twenty to twenty-five repetitions and single set. Don't do too many at first or you'll be sore the next day. Increase your repetitions gradually until you are able to do two sets, or forty to fifty repetitions each.

3. *Sit-ups.* Sit-ups can be done on the floor, on an inclined plane, or even on a stool with your feet hooked. The choice depends on your current fitness level and the equipment at hand. If you travel, you can hook your feet under the motel bed. An easier way is to lie flat with your feet drawn up about a foot from your buttocks. Fold your arms over your chest and

raise your body up towards your knees, then lower it slowly. Do as many of these as you can without excessive strain. You can, if you like, hold each one for a few seconds at the point where your back is off the floor. These are called "cramp sit-ups." I personally prefer full-range sit-ups, in which your legs are slightly bent and you move over a full arc. Work up to about fifty full-range sit-ups.

4. *Push-ups.* This exercise has endless variations, from the knees or the toes, with palms flat or on the fists. You can spread your arms wide, keep them narrow, or place them about shoulder width. You can use two hands or one and do them fast or slow. For starters, I recommend that you keep your palms flat and placed slightly narrower than shoulder width. Your back should be straight, and if possible, only your hands and toes should be touching the floor. Lower your body, keeping it straight at all times, allow your chest to touch the floor, and then raise your body again until your arms are extended but not locked. Begin with a single set, however many you can do comfortably in correct form. Build until you can do twenty-five repetitions without stopping, then gradually add a second set, and a third. Three sets done in this manner will do much for your upper-body tone.

5. *Isometric supplements.* These are exercises in which you apply pressure against a stationary object such as a wall. I'm not fond of these for the simple reason that most people forget to breathe when they do them. This places an inordinate strain on the heart. **If** you remember to breathe, however, there are several isometrically based exercises that are without risk. You can do a curl with one hand while resisting with the other. You can climb an imaginary rope by pulling one-hand down while you resist with the other. You can do tricep (outer upper arm) exercises by bringing one hand down in an arc from the opposite shoulder while resisting with the other hand. The possibilities are endless. You can develop your own routine depending on the muscle groups you want to exercise.

6. *Cooling down.* Calisthenics can leave you with a feeling of tightness and a temporary oxygen/carbon-dioxide inbalance. It is important, therefore, to allow your body to cool down gradually and expel excess carbon dioxide. Your cool-down

should include mild jumping jacks, walking around briskly and then slowly, and swinging your arms from side to side. Just be sure to keep moving until you feel completely relaxed and your pulse rate is regular. You might want to end with two minutes of breath cleansing.

Calisthenics should be in addition your aerobic exercises. If you exercise aerobically, you should also do two muscle routines a week, preferably not on your aerobics days.[4] These need not take longer than thirty minutes each.

Weight Training. You may prefer free weight or Nautilus training as a supplement to your aerobics conditioning (I do both). If so, I strongly recommend that you join a health club. If you prefer Nautilus, you will almost certainly have to join a club, because the equipment is quite expensive. Even if you plan to exercise at home, the instruction is well worth the money. In either case, here are some principles you might keep in mind:

1. *Begin with the largest muscle groups and progress to the smaller ones.* The correct order is: lower back, abdominals, upper back and shoulders, triceps, biceps, forearms, and wrists. Working the larger groups first increases the flow of blood to the muscle tissue and minimizes the risk of injury that can occur when the smaller muscles are fatigued excessively.

2. *Progress gradually.* Begin with light weights and a single set of exercises for each muscle group, and gradually progress to three sets. Don't do too much at first. You will become sore and discouraged.

3. *Balance sets and repetitions.* A "set" is a specified number of repetitions of a single exercise completed without stopping.

[4]There's been much attention given lately to circuit training, that is weight training exercises done in a precise order and at a certain speed so as to promote a sustained elevated heart rate. I'm sure circuit training has its followers and I don't want to discourage them. Any exercise is better than none. I will only say, having spent nearly forty years heaving weights around, that for me, circuit training is an unacceptable compromise. It appears to promise both aerobic and muscular fitness in less time than it would normally take to achieve either. My own observation of circuit training is that it attracts many people who want to get their workouts over with as quickly as possible. In fitness training, as in most other things, you get out of it what you put in it.

You should progress to multiple sets because it is difficult to tire a conditioned muscle with only one set. Doing too many repetitions can produce excessive muscle fatigue. Generally, you should use a weight that allows eight to ten repetitions if you want to build muscle, or ten to twelve if you want only tone and endurance. For the larger muscle groups (legs, back, and abdominals), increase ranges to ten to twelve and twelve to fifteen, respectively, since these groups are more powerful and do not fatigue as easily.

If you want to build (as opposed to simply toning) the muscles, you'll probably require three workouts a week with a day between each for your aerobic workouts. You can expect to do fewer workouts with weights than with calisthenics, and fewer with Nautilus than with free weights. Even with Nautilus, many trainers recommend three sessions a week.

4. *Breathe.* This may seem funny, but a lot of people forget to breathe when they exercise. They hold their breath while they're lifting and put unnecessary strain on the heart. Breathe, and breathe abdominally.

5. *Alternate aerobic and muscular workouts.* If possible, avoid doing aerobic and weight exercise on the same day. If you must do them in a single day, do your weight workout first. This is especially important if you run. Running causes tenderness and mild joint inflammation. Following running with weight training increases your chances of injury.

6. *Don't skip muscle groups or work only one side of the body.* Seek balance in your routine. Get the blood flowing throughout you entire body and exercise every muscle group. Overworking one side of the body, unless you are undergoing corrective therapy, is a poor practice.

7. *Avoid excess strain.* Once you begin weight training, you may be inclined to push yourself. This is fine up to a point, but excessive strain can cause injury and actually reduce muscle size. If your muscles are constantly sore after the first few weeks, you're doing too much. Some soreness is natural, but to be hobbling around in pain all of the time is foolish.

If you're injured, back off. Allow the injury a chance to heal, and seek professional guidance regarding your exercise routine. Don't develop your own corrective exercises and hope they will work. Ask someone who knows.

Getting Started

You now have the basics for developing a program. You're aiming at no fewer than three exercise periods a week, preferably five, and you recognize that aerobic training comes first. Thus, if you do only three workouts, they should all be aerobic. Try to keep your aerobic and muscular workouts separate, although you may if you prefer, add calisthenics to your running after you run. Now, before you head off for the gym or the track, consider these questions:

Do I need a physical exam? If you're over thirty-five and in poor condition, probably yes. If you do decide to have one, look for a specialist in sports medicine. Most local running clubs keep lists of them. If your physician doesn't exercise regularly himself, smokes, or can't see over his belt buckle, get another one! And, if you're more than fifteen or twenty pounds over weight, insist on a stress EEG test as part of your physical.

Should I take a fitness test? If you're out of shape, such a test could be dangerous. Better to wait until you have exercised regularly for a month or so. Frankly, I think that most fitness tests are simply ego trips. As a general rule, I don't think they're necessary or advisable.

The Role of Diet

Next to sex and the economy, diet is our most popular subject. The list of diet books is almost endless. There are some good ones and many very poor ones.[5] Rather than discussing the merits of any particular diet, let's concentrate on some fundamental principles. These are things you can apply yourself.

Nutrient groups. You'll recall that everything we eat can be grouped into three basic categories: fats, proteins, and carbohydrates. The average American's diet consists of 46 percent

---

[5]One brief and excellent book is *Fit or Fat*, by Covert Bailey. In just over a hundred pages, Bailey presents a concise discussion of the relationships between food, exercise, and the body. Also, for general reference, I recommend the *Nutrition Almanac*.

carbohydrates, 12 percent proteins, and 42 percent fats. As you know, excess proteins cannot be stored. They pass right through the system. You'll recall also that excess carbohydrates are ultimately converted to fat.

There is considerable evidence that our current 'alance of proteins, fats, and carbohydrates is inappropriate. The Senate Select Committee on Nutrition has recommended a decrease in the amount of fat consumed of at least 12 percent. As a practical matter, it's almost impossible to get too little fat in your diet if you are an American. The committee recommended that complex carbohydrates such as are found in fresh fruits and vegetables be increased to 58 percent. The important thing is to reduce the proportion of high-cholesterol fatty substances that are so much a part of the American eating plan.

How much should you eat? Well, it requires 12 to 15 calories to maintain one pound of bodyweight. So if you weigh 150 pounds, you will have to eat between 1,800 and 2,250 calories a day to maintain your weight. This depends, of course, on the amount of exercise you get. Exercise alone will not enable you to lose weight. Remember, depending on your weight, running a mile in eight minutes will enable you to burn up approximately 125 calories.

Both diet and exercise are required if you want to lose weight. Exercise increases metabolic effectiveness. It helps your body process and convert food efficiently and, contrary to popular belief, does not increase your appetite. In fact, just the reverse is true. Moderate exercise actually curbs appetite.

Let's assume you want to lose weight. What principles can you follow? Keep these in mind:

1. *Reduce calories and maintain a balanced diet.* This means a diet that is low in simple carbohydrates (such as sugars); high in protein; low in fats (one to three teaspoons of polyunsaturated per day); heavy on liquid (six to seven glasses daily); light in refined sugar; and rich in complex carbohydrates such as those found in fresh fruits, natural grains, and vegetables.

2. *Maintain a minimum caloric level.* Ideally, you don't want to lose more than one or two pounds a week. Diets that allow less than 1,000 calories a day should be avoided.

3. *Eat slowly.* Most of us gulp our food, chew too fast, and take far too big bites. This is hard on the digestive system and encourages overeating. Since it requires thirty minutes for your stomach to acknowledge the food it receives, you can easily overeat and not know it. I find that eating slowly is an excellent way to curb this tendency. A chewing rate of approximately thirty chews a minute will force you to slow down and appreciate your food. Try timing yourself with a stopwatch. Build a slow relaxed rhythm in your chewing. If you have a metronome for your piano days, use it. Develop a habit of eating slowly.

4. *Set an upper weight limit and stick to it.* Generally about five pounds above your desired weight should be your limit. Most people vary naturally up to three pounds due to climatic changes, sleeping habits, menstrual periods, and exercise variations. When you reach your limit, cut your intake. I find a simple method for these minidiets is to eliminate butter, sugar, bread, candy, and all desserts. This means no sweets of any kind until I reach my desired weight. This works well and is easy to do.

5. *If you feel dizzy, check your caloric intake.* Be sure you have not cut your intake too much. While I do not normally advise vitamin supplements, it is sometimes wise to take a multiple vitamin and iron supplement when you are dieting for any significant period of time, particularly if you experience dizziness or nausea. If you feel nauseous, it probably means you are loosing too fast or failing to maintain a balanced diet.

6. *Avoid fad diets.* I'm talking here about diets that offer rapid weight loss by radically unbalancing the metabolic system. These include very low carbohydrate, water flooding, and the kelp-vinegar diets. The key lies in permanently changing your eating habits so that you don't need to diet. This means reducing caloric intake to a level appropriate to the weight you want to maintain, given your activity level, and following a balanced healthy diet.

Once you have brought your weight down to where you want it, there are simple practices you can follow, in addition to chewing slowly, setting limits, and maintaining a correct balance. I suggest the following:

- Restrict red meats to twice a week.
- Avoid or significantly curtail consumption of the four whites: white flour, white sugar, white rice, and salt.
- Eliminate or severely restrict your intake of caffeine in coffee, tea, and colas. I believe that caffeine buildup in the body reduces it's resistance to disease.
- If you get hungry, eat a piece of fruit or a slice of raw vegetable thirty minutes before dinner.
- Make exercise a regular part of your life, but time your workouts so that you do not exercise strenuously sooner than ninety minutes after, or thirty minutes before, a meal.

If you follow these practices, you'll find it easier to maintain proper weight and you'll feel better. Our habits of overeating and underexercising have dulled our sensibilities. You are retuning the body so that it can advise you properly.

I've failed to mention two subjects that are on nearly everyone's list: alcohol and tobacco. There is mounting evidence that light or moderate use of alcohol is not harmful and may be beneficial. Beer, for example, has been found to increase the kidney washing function for marathon runners who dehydrate so quickly in warm climates that water never reaches their kidneys during a race. Alcohol, in moderate amounts, clearly relaxes. Current findings differ, but a maximum of two ounces of eighty-proof alcohol per day seems to be the dividing line between healthful and unhealthful imbibing. If you exercise and meditate regularly and eat sensibly, you probably won't want that much. The important thing is moderation.

I wish I could tell you that similar guidelines apply to smoking. They **don't!** If you smoke, you're greatly increasing your chances of getting a variety of painful fatal diseases. In this case, moderation is not a solution. If you smoke a pack a day, you are three times more likely to suffer a heart attack than is a nonsmoker. You will die younger and suffer longer fighting cancer, emphysema, or a stroke. And it is *not* necessarily true that if you stop, the lungs will repair in a few years. One man I knew who had been a heavy smoker hadn't smoked for over twenty-five years. He contracted cancer and died despite all efforts to save him. The attending surgeon commented afterward to his wife, "Your husband must have been a heavy smoker. His lungs were nearly gone." The fact is, your body reflects what you do to it or for it.

Fitness and Discovery

It **pays** to be fit. You live better, feel more alive, and you may live longer. It is tragic that so many people gauge their well-being by comparing their chronological ages with norms, for the "average" normal person declines far earlier and faster than necessary. It is possible to be active and fit well into advanced age. The later years do not have to be ones of decline, disease, and immobility. They can be rich in growth and discovery.

Perhaps the best reason for being fit is the one I suggested earlier: physical fitness supports the mind/body partnership that enables you to reach your full potential. The vastly increased awareness that results from this partnership is an essential element in the warrior philosophy. Being a warrior means being totally prepared and fit.

Once again, we're going to shift gears rapidly. These past four chapters have been concerned with technique, the "how to" of discovering the warrior spirit. Now, we're going to turn to the end result—the nature of the discovered self and the qualities it includes, some strategies for living that are implicit in these qualities, and some examples of discoveries that flow naturally from realizing these qualities in your experience. My intent, in these final chapters, is to give you a sense of the tremendous benefits that can be realized by following the approaches we've discussed.

CHAPTER SEVEN
THE DISCOVERED SELF

C hapter 2 described the constructed self. That is the self, you'll recall, that promises consistency and certainty at a sacrifice of accuracy and truth. It is the self that leaves us controlled rather than in control, victims of bitterness, guilt, resentment, and style. It exacts a steep price for the dubious benefits it bestows.

Most of us eventually outgrow the constructed self. Consistency gives way to the world of opposites. The healthy person is often a maze of contradictions. In fact, psychologists have noted that well-balanced people tend to display paradoxical or opposite qualities.[1] They can be, for example, both bold and cautious, childlike and mature, gentle and tough. To their closest friends, they often appear unpredictable and full of contrasts.

I've confirmed these observations with hundreds of seminar participants. The presence of seemingly irreconcilable opposites in healthy people has been confirmed in just about every group surveyed. These contrasting facets reveal the person in transition, shifting gradually or abruptly from the constructed world of reaction and pattern to a different base of awareness. It is this changed awareness that we will be discussing as we consider a new kind of self—the discovered self.

The discovered qualities emerge gently over time, not as improvements in the old constructed self, but as rebirth, as new being. They are the heart of the warrior's philosophy, the driving force behind the ceaseless quest for self-knowledge.

[1]Dr. Lawrence Siebert, one of the reviewers of this book and a longtime colleague, has been working with the idea of paradoxical qualities for several years. His forthcoming book, *The Survivor Personality*, discusses the role of opposite qualities in survivors and points out that people who are good survivors gain strength from adversities they deal with.

They inspire you to shun the mundane and reach for excellence, and they awaken you to the need for strategies that protect and further the discovery process. Let's look at the process, the qualities, and the strategies in turn.

The Discovery Process

How do the discovered qualities appear and what can you do to make them happen? How can you be sure they're not simply different facets of the constructed self?

Discovery, like creativity, is a matter of preparation. Transformation occurs when you are ready, prepared. Sometimes it happens suddenly; more often it occurs gradually and goes almost unnoticed. The qualities we'll be discussing appeared in my life over the past ten years. They are derived from experience, but not mine alone. I've met others who have made similar discoveries and who confirm the gradualness of the discovery process. It cannot be forced.

But it **can** be encouraged. The steps I've described earlier—writing your own history, centering, meditation, and reopening the mind-body dialogue—are preparation. Taken together, they lead the way without dictating the result. They expand awareness and render the mind more open and willing to respond. As I noted earlier, you won't be convinced of this by argument or logic. The proof lies in **doing.** I can only describe what I've found and how it has worked for me and others. You must prove it for yourself.

I've chosen to describe the discovered self in terms of eight qualities. There could have been ten or maybe more. Any single quality includes and suggests others. Openness, for example, one of the eight, includes curiosity. Exhilaration, another, inspires a sense of humor. The number, eight, like language itself, is a matter of convenience, a limited approach to a limitless topic.

As you think about these qualities, you may want to adapt them to your own needs, change some and add others. That's good. For now, however, they provide the structure and metaphor that allow us to share the universality of our respective experiences. If you find there are places where we **don't** agree (and there may well be), you may be discovering that each of us enjoys his or her own beautiful uniqueness, and that too is as it should be.

The Discovered Qualities

The first five qualities we'll be discussing emerged more or less chronologically in my experience. For example, stillness, the first of the eight, led to increasing inner-directedness, which, in turn, caused me to open up and become more gentle with myself and others. Once I began to look beyond the constructed, outer-directed self, I became inexplicably exhilarated by what I saw.

The last three qualities appeared randomly and seemed to weave in and out among the others. For example, I gradually became comfortable with ideas and attitudes that would have been intolerable only a few years earlier. On the other hand, I became impatient with views I had tolerated or even welcomed before. Accompanying those feelings was a growing sense of being part of a higher order. Controlling and leading became less important than listening and obeying. Throughout the process and the decade, the journey remained highly personal, seldom shared or understood by those around me. By this, you may conclude correctly that discovery can be a lonely process! Do *not* be deterred by criticism or ridicule of your search. You will undoubtedly encounter much resistance as you discover that the warrior often travels alone. Now let's look at the eight qualities.

Stillness. You would think that it would be easy to be still. You think you need only get off where it's quiet, relax, and let it happen. Unfortunately that is not always the case.

I knew a woman, mother of two and a loser in two successive marriages, physically beautiful, but emotionally wracked and torn. She filled her days with people, work, and noise, anything to avoid being alone. She was unhappy, plagued with problems, and badly in need of someone to talk with. I urged her to take half an hour each day and go out, sit on a rock, and do nothing. She made up excuses. She was always too busy or too tired. When she finally yielded after two months of urging, she all but ran from her rock when the time was up. It was nearly a year before she could stand to be alone with herself again.

Why do people fear silence and want to fill each moment with talking or moving about? They seem terrified by times when nothing's happening. I noticed this in others long before I saw it in myself.

It's natural to avoid introspection, to lose oneself in externals. When the pressure becomes too great, the usual approach is to talk, argue, defend, or attack. Take a vacation or find a new mate. Feel abused and put upon because "others" are doing it to you. Place the blame out there and avoid looking inside. But the crux of the matter is that it's **not** out there. The problem and the solution are both within.

During a period when things weren't going well at all, I used to jog in a park by the Potomac River. There were huge rocks, waterfalls, and half a mile of rapids. I would stop and sit for hours on a rock trying to sort things out. I would meditate, sometimes on a problem, sometimes on a mantra, counting, or just on a point in my thought. One afternoon I climbed to a ledge overlooking a small pool. The water's calm surface reflected clouds, trees, and a flight of wood ducks heading west. Each movement was mirrored instantly. I threw a pebble into the pool and watched the ripples radiating out in perfect circles. The water gradually subsided and the surface became calm again. Then it dawned on me—the pool was my inner self, the part of me that waited quietly and responded instantly, effortlessly, and appropriately. I can rediscover my center only as I go into this inner stillness, this original place. I must forsake tradition, teaching, and dogma and attend to the inner voice. Then I become the eye of the hurricane, the center that is part of a larger order and harmony. Stillness is the key to it all.

Stillness is not so much a place to go as something you're part of. It is the anteroom of the inner self. You achieve it not by seeking, but by recognizing. It can only be partly understood through explanation and metaphor. To be fully known, it must be experienced, partaken of, and the way to experience it is to do it. Getting off alone and meditating sets the stage and provides an atmosphere free of distraction. It's a way to trigger the discovery process.

Going off and sitting on a rock can be a threat to others. It's a sure way to be accused of being selfish. Mothers especially are made to feel guilty. They give of their milk and their time until they are simply facilitators for their children and husbands. Before long they are convinced that taking time for themselves is just being selfish.

It may seem strange that going off alone can be a selfless act. The reason is that you aren't prepared to give your best until you discover who you are and what your best *is*. The wife who spends all of her waking hours with children, neighbors, and husband feels drained. She is. She has lost touch with what she really is. The husband wedded to his office and his briefcase has forgotten what he is all about. Both owe it to themselves to get away, to look deep inside at what they really are and what they have to give.

It takes courage to demand time for yourself. At first glance, it may seem to be the ultimate in selfishness, a real slap in the face to those who love and depend on you. It's not. It means you care enough to want to see the best in yourself and give only the best to others. It is silent recognition that your obligation to them is to give your best, and *nothing less*.

Inner-directedness. Stillness is the path to inner-directedness. It reveals the inner compass and gyro that chart the course and maintain balance. For some, this guidance comes easily; for others, it can be a struggle.

An early psychologist named Gustav Fechner built a lopsided frame and placed a rod inside. The rod was straight, cleanly vertical, but because of the frame, it appeared to lean. He showed it to friends and found that some could not be fooled. They saw the rod as it was, not as it appeared to be. They weren't influenced by the frame at all. They were what Fechner called "field independent." Such people, he found, tended to be independent of other things—their surroundings, other people, habitual patterns, and so on. His research seems to imply that independence is an inborn trait. I'm not so sure. There was a time when I *didn't* have it . . .

We are in the air, eighteen hundred feet above the ground in my Piper PA-12. It's exam day, the day I test for my pilot's license. I'm in front, my instructor is in the rear. He's a gruff giant of a man who began flying as a barnstormer in the twenties. Now he's just a pilot–instructor–airport operator, staid in these his later years, but still showing signs of wilder days—assorted scars and a metal plate in his head, souvenirs of two crashes.

We climb up into the sky. He gives me a course, sits back sullenly, and says nothing for what seems to be an eternity. Then, from the back seat, "Turn the key off." Obediently, I give away that comfortable sound of safety, the steady drone that tells me all is well. Now there is only the windmilling prop. "Why doesn't it stop?" he asks.

"I don't know. I guess it's the wind."

"Right," he says. "Raise the nose. Pull back on the stick." I do as he says and the prop stops, vertically, so that it splits my vision and reminds me that it too has quit.

"All right. Find a field and land." I look around and carefully maneuver the plane so I can see to the rear. Now we're down to sixteen hundred feet. Ah, there's a field dead ahead, about six miles away. Is it long enough? Can I make it? Yes, I think so.

"Where the hell are you going?" he yells.

"Over there, to the field by the road," I stammer.

"Look below you. No! Not there, right under the plane . . . See it?" There, directly below, is an emergency field, eighteen hundred feet long, neatly mowed, just the thing. I spiral down and carefully, oh so carefully, land dead stick.

We sit quietly in silence, then he begins: "Always look directly below you when the engine quits. Chances are there's a field nearby that will do. Don't look away off and head for the farthest one away. Jesus. Half my students do that. It's stupid."

Years later the lesson is still fresh in my mind. Many of us spend our lives looking into the distance, missing what's right at hand. We formulate goals, strive for success, and think that getting there must be an arduous process. Like Fechner's subjects, we are bound by the form and history of our surroundings, culture, and habits. We lack the spontaneity of unpatterned thinking and living.

It's easy to become swayed by your surroundings, to view the world as others do, or as they want you to. If you don't

watch out, you'll begin believing that you must look old to be
mature, or that you need wear a dark suit to be an executive. If
your skin or eyes are the wrong color, you may become convinced you're inferior. And if you grew up in a tough neighbor-
hood, you may feel that you still come from the wrong side of
the tracks.

Not caring about what others think is great if you're rich
and single. For others, it can be a drag. Being out of step with
the majority can be tiring, but sometimes it's necessary. You
reach a point where truth becomes more important than
conformity. The problem is that then it's awfully easy to react
and be captured. You blame others for your dilemma and look
outside for solutions. You're even less likely to trust in yourself
because you've challenged the existing order and found the
going tough.

Sometimes though, the inner leading prevails. It may be
only a minor incident, but it tells you you're on the right path.
Once our son came into the kitchen to ask permission to go
somewhere or do something, I don't recall which. Carol stopped
him in mid-sentence and told him that—of course he could not.
Here were all the whys and wherefores. I wondered, "What's
wrong with me? Why don't I have such ready answers?" I felt
uncomfortable. A firm "no" is probably better than a doubtful
"yes." I said nothing, and the decision stood. Yet, deep down
inside, I sensed that I was beginning to see things differently,
that some old ways were crumbling.

It takes a while to learn to follow your inner leadings.
You're called upon to explain your logic when you have none
or defend your intuition when you aren't sure of it. You argue
even though you sense that argument is no longer appropriate.
This seesawing continues until you learn to listen for the inner
voice and rely on it. Initially, I found it easier to depend on
intuition for little things, like recovering lost articles, sensing
others' thoughts, or choosing the right road on a trip. Gradually,
with practice, my confidence, awareness, and accuracy improved and I began to trust the inner voice on larger issues.

Openness. The genuinely open person sees things as they
are not as they should be. He or she is present oriented, concerned with what IS.

Openness is essential to growth. Narrow your eyes and squint with hard focus, and you see less. Close your mind, and you narrow your perspective. Close your fists, and you cannot receive the gift. For the person who wants to grow, openness is the only way, but it has its dangers.

Many people still equate openness with weakness. Tipping your hand in cards or in life leaves you vulnerable. The candidate who tells voters frankly how little he or she knows about an issue can be attacked. Executives who show their people that they care face increased pressure in the next round of wage negotiations—or so the traditional wisdom has it.

Openness based on will **is** weakness. Resolve without understanding is like a bad bluff in poker; if it's challenged, you're in trouble. To resolve to be more open with yourself, your spouse, or your associates is to miss the point. Openness results from an increased awareness that only the present counts. The truly open person is not frightened by what might be. He or she focuses attention on NOW, realizing that the future can only be altered by what is achieved in the present. Openness **happens**; it cannot be made to happen. It evolves naturally out of being centered and inner-directed. You can decide you want to be open, but that won't make it so. It only happens when you **see** that it's the only way. This kind of openness is honesty and power.

A friend of mine is young in his eighties. He's more open than most children I've known, and they're usually the best examples. We'll call him Carl, so as not to embarrass him. I've noticed over the years that when Carl gets involved in an argument with someone (he doesn't argue, **they** do), he always hesitates before he answers. Sometimes he'll look the other person directly in the eye. More often he seems to be staring slightly above their head. Then he'll reply, and what he says is usually right on target, well put, and calmly said. I asked him what was happening in those moments of silence. "Oh," he replied, "I'm just trying to get Carl out of the way so that I can hear what the other fellow's really saying."

Carl possesses a rare kind of openness. He isn't affected by what others say, only by what IS, and he has learned to distinguish between the two. He has no private skeletons in his closet and refuses to let anybody put them there. He is convinced that every person and incident is drawn to him to teach him more. At somewhere on the other side of eighty, he is eager and open to learn. He has power that many of us lack.

Gentleness. Women are supposed to be gentle, and men tough. If you're a man, unless you're 6' 5" and weigh 260 pounds, gentleness is regarded as weakness. For a long time, it seems, we can't afford to be gentle. We're too busy proving ourselves, showing we can take it, and scrambling to the top. It's tragic that, for many, gentleness comes only with age and sometimes not even then.

I discovered gentleness the hard way, by hurting people. When you're accustomed to competing, you learn to overcome obstacles. If they're people, you go around, over, or through them. You want your kids and your wife to be tough, so you constantly try to teach them. You mistake their occasional resistance for strength, when often it's fear, and you hurt them. Even when you realize what you're doing, you're so accustomed to fighting that you can't back off. You just keep boring in.

Two dogs ambled by the house one morning, a big German shepherd and a miniature schnauzer. Farther up the road, coming toward them, was a large and threatening Doberman. As it got closer, the Doberman headed directly for the schnauzer, its eyes focused on the hair on its neck bristling. The schnauzer froze, petrified by what it saw. The shepherd, meanwhile, positioned itself between the two dogs and then began a kind of dance. Each time the Doberman moved toward the schnauzer, the shepherd would block its advance. Finally, in frustration, the Doberman charged. The shepherd shifted its position ever so slightly, hit the Doberman broadside, and calmly stood its ground, making no effort to follow up using its obvious advantage. After one more futile attempt, the Doberman turned and went back up the road.

Why does it take us so long to see the obvious?: gentleness requires tremendous strength. Gentleness is having the power **not** to react when everything about the circumstance says you should. Gentleness is the beginning of learning what love is all about. How does it happen? What finally turns the light on?

For me, it wasn't until I'd begun to open my eyes and look around, as Carl did, and see behind the defenses people put up to conceal their real needs. When I learned to open up, to risk being hurt, I began to understand what it means to hurt others.

The gentle person is the more aware person. He or she goes behind the facade and beneath the surface to heal rather than hurt. I'm convinced that gentleness is a prerequisite of intuition, which is simply seeing in a different way, with more than the eyes. My intuition tells me that, in most instances, hurting people doesn't make sense.

Exhilaration. Henry Thoreau observed that "the mass of men lead lives of quiet desperation." That was long ago and much has changed since then, but there are still too many people who are angry and frustrated, and they aren't all poor either. There are many reasons for being unhappy, and most of them are of our own doing. The simple fact that we realize if we think about it is that money, position, and prestige do not guarantee happiness. Success for many people is indefinable and illusive. For them, gains are counterbalanced by losses, with predictably mediocre results.

Exhilaration is joy, often over small things and sometimes without apparent reason. I recall walking down our driveway in Virginia one spring morning. The grass sparkled with sunlit dew. Birds sang noisily, and billowy cumulous clouds drifted across the sky. I stopped, stunned by the overwhelming beauty. My whole body seemed charged with energy, my chest nearly bursting, my arms powerful, and my mind clear and brilliant. I wanted to scream with delight.

It took time to learn that not everyone feels this way, not even occasionally. Many are so burdened by the past or threatened by the future that the present holds only sparse joys. Yet exhilaration **is** part of the true self. It is discovered only as we look for it. It requires forsaking of the rational, rebirth, access to new heights. There are lots of ways to get it. Some get their highs from climbing mountains, others from racing cars. I get some of mine from flying, like that day on the way back from Wilmington . . .

"Wilmington Aviation Weather. Ceiling five hundred, overcast, tops six thousand. Visibility one mile, rain and fog.

Wind two-seven-zero at ten. Temperature three-four, dewpoint three-two. Light rime icing in clouds."

"Wilmington Departure. 8603 Quebec, IFR Dulles, on our way to eight thousand." I leave the narrow ribbon of clear air and ascend into a bed of white formless clouds. Wisps of rain freeze on the windshield as the Beech Bonanza climbs through the overcast. We are alone, plane and I, returning to our home base at Dulles International. The ascent is smooth, the wind unnoticeable in the warm protected cockpit greenhouse.

The white clouds are grey, dulled by nearly six thousand feet of thickness. Then they begin to lighten. There's a hole above and suddenly I'm in the clear. Now there is only bright blue sky, soft beds of white, and glistening sunlight. I'm free!

There are many thrills in flying, and this is one of them: breaking out of a solid overcast into the bright sun alone, pilot and plane. The earth seems far below, unimportant, part of yesterday. Now all that matters is the brightness, the blue, and the bed of white two thousand feet below. I know rather than feel the motion. It's almost as though time has ceased to exist.

I thrive on highs, momentary injections of adrenalin that send me skyrocketing into the heights. Flying is one of those highs. Not in a big commercial jet with all of the comforts and protections of organized transport, but in a ship I can get my hands on and become part of. The Bonanza is one of those planes. Any pilot will tell you. The majestic V-tail gives a gentle oscillation in the roughest of weather, rocks you like a baby in a crib. There's security in the cockpit, a bond between pilot and machine. There are moments when I can feel the motion throughout my entire body, when mystically I become the plane, sense its mood, know its speed and direction, and share its power.

We all need to fly, need our own special kind of freedom, our highs. Something that puts a distance between us and the rest of humanity, between living and existing. Life without natural highs is hardly more than mere existence. I've had similar highs while running, while standing on a narrow precipice at fourteen thousand feet, while shussing a ski run at top speed, and while gazing silently at the hills above Cape Cod Bay at sunset. Highs come in different shapes and sizes, all of them natural and real. I don't need drugs or booze, and it doesn't matter whether highs are in a plane, on a hill, or in my living room. What matters is that they happen.

We learn through highs. Exhilaration is the beginning of discovering the power available to us. It is the incipient awareness that we are not simply accidental bumps on life's road, but part of a larger purpose.

A capacity to entertain untraditional views. It's natural to label others with ready-made terms. Referring to someone as a conservative, a Catholic, or a bank president helps describe that person. It also makes it more difficult to see him or her as a person.

With increasing inner-directedness, the inadequacy of traditional labeling becomes obvious. The more you learn about yourself, the more likely you are to see others clearly. This increased clarity can be as shocking as looking at a drop of water through a microscope for the first time. You see things as they are rather than as you thought they were. Sometimes a friend you've known for years begins to look like a different person.

Tradition provides labels at the expense of truth. Much tradition survives only by weight of repetition, not by force of truth. That me and mine are enlightened and you and yours are not is nonsense, yet I believed it once. I felt that my religion and my church were the full and final word. Now I don't. I keep bumping into added bits of truth in strange places.

Having a capacity to hear untraditional views doesn't just mean tolerating them; it means understanding them. It means putting myself in your place so I can see why you think the way you do. Until I'm willing to do that, I will never fully understand you. I'll remain convinced you're wrong, when maybe I am the one who is off base.

What causes either of us to open up, to ask questions instead of always having answers? What tells me that I can learn from you and from everyone else I meet? Remember Carl, who stopped to get himself out of the way before answering? I think I became willing to question traditional wisdom when I stopped to listen, when I started asking questions and really heard the answers. That took time, and it was all involved with being still, open, inner-directed, gentle, and exhilarated. And I didn't just decide to be different. I tried that years before and it didn't work. My attitudes changed when I was prepared to accept a new perspective.

Being receptive to the new or different is important, but it can be risky. You'll be told you're wrong, and tradition has it that being wrong is bad. Being right is better and safer. The man or woman who risks being wrong goes against the majority and is applauded only when the majority comes around. But the greater risk lies in being unwilling to risk. Mistakes are simply lessons we haven't yet learned. Being wrong may be a necessary step in proving truth for oneself. In that case, right or wrong is insignificant in terms of the final outcome. It's just another correction in which we're off course much of the time, but always adjusting and coming nearer the truth. Risk is a cost of growth.

Impatience with the banal. I was taught that patience is a virtue. Better to wait for the moving of the water than wade right in and muddy the whole creekbed. Consequently, it came as a surprise when, midstream at forty-one, I discovered I'd been impatient for a long time. I felt that my life should be working better and was frustrated that it wasn't. I knew that forcing things often only made matters worse, but when push came to shove, I was right there in the pack trying to improve the bottom line and salt away the bucks.

Then in the midst of a particularly difficult crisis, I resolved to find out what was bugging me. What I learned was so simple it startled me: for years I had been willing to settle for less than my best. I had sought money and power without realizing that those goals really limited my growth and understanding.

Years earlier, someone had warned me, but I wasn't listening. I was a management consultant attending a Saturday morning training session on business development and personal incentives. The managing director of the office sat next to me. He listened as each person spoke, and then he addressed the group as a whole: "The money you're making isn't important. The only thing that *is* important is your own excellence. If you are really outstanding, the money will come." The director's annual income on that Saturday morning was just about ten times my own. "Fine," I thought to myself. "That's easy for you to say. You've got it made." Fifteen years later when all hell was breaking loose, I learned he was right.

It's often difficult to focus on what's important. It's easier to become caught up in trivia—more money, a bigger house, more expensive cars and planes. Before long, trivia invades every corner of your life. You tolerate endless meetings, mounds of paperwork, and insipid cocktail parties. You become a patient audience for anyone who wants to bend your ear.

Being intolerant of the banal takes courage at first. Banality, like tradition, is supported by the majority. Eventually, however, refusing to accept banality in your life becomes essential. There is so much to do, so much to learn, that every moment becomes precious. The significance of life begins to assert itself and impatience becomes a virtue.

Awareness of a higher conformity. Conforming has become a bad word. Being an iconoclast and breaking all of the rules is regarded by many as the mark of an independent thinker. But what of the avowed nonconformist who stands on his head just to be different? Hasn't he been taken captive by a worse kind of conformity?

The answer, it seems to me, is not whether you conform, but to **what** you choose to conform. Jesus was an intelligent nonconformist, crucified by his own people for violating their rules. It took an outsider to see what the Jews had missed. A centurion who asked Jesus to heal his servant of palsy observed, "For I also am a man set under authority. . . ." He saw that Jesus conformed to a higher law.

This awareness of higher law and of the necessity of conforming to it is implicit in the discovered self. This law is neither civil nor canonical. It is the fundamental law of being, perceived directly and requiring no intermediaries to interpret or enforce. For one who embraces the warrior spirit, the highest goal is to find and follow this law. This kind of conformity bestows real power. It was the object of Jesus' mission, as he explained to his mother when she chastened him for preaching in the temple: "Son, why hast thou thus dealt with us?" she asked. Jesus answered her: "How is it that ye sought me? Wist

114

ye not that I must be about my Father's business?" He recognized his mission and, at age twelve, refused to be dissuaded from it.

Essential Strategies

The discovered qualities reinforce one another, each adding to a growing recognition that we all have a higher calling. It is important that we protect this growing awareness. You'll recall the distinction made in Chapter 4 between real and apparent power. I noted then that apparent power is never neutral, that it always assumes borrowed forms and seeks to control. Apparent power tries to undermine what we are and what we can be. You can protect your understanding by employing strategies that complement the discovered qualities. For me, these strategies developed spontaneously over the past decade. I've termed them the warrior strategies, and there are twelve of them. Study them. Test them for yourself. Here they are.

1. *Guard the self.* The conditions that encourage the appearance of the discovered self are subtle and delicate. The world seems to be for noise and against silence. Finding stillness, going off regularly to be alone with your thoughts takes courage. Becoming inner-directed sometimes requires that you refuse direction from others, not overtly or brazenly, but gently and imperceptibly. Guarding the self is like balancing a glass of water on a stick; it requires precision and constant attention. Guarding the self through meditation, or writing, or running is not selfishness; it is a requirement of excellence.

2. *Assume responsibility.* You are responsible for *your* actions, thoughts, emotions, and destiny. While you are responsible for the effects of your actions *upon* others, you are *not* responsible for others themselves. In accepting responsibility for others, you may be depriving them of their chance to grow.

We are not responsible **for** others, but we are responsible **to** them. Our responsibilities to others are the same as those to ourselves: to allow them the same awareness, self-discovery, and completeness that we claim for ourselves. This can be difficult if they don't see it for themselves. But seeing it for them, silently, heals.

3. *Test all authorities.* Human authorities are fallible. Beware of parent, priest, or potentate who tells you what truth is. Odds are he or she is bluffing, and both of you are being taken in. Truth results from discovery more than instruction. What is true for me may not be true for you. The test for each of us is that it squares with our inner sense of right. My truth and your truth may be different tomorrow. It must be if we are growing, and growth is the *one* inviolable law.

4. *Trust in yourself, not in others.* Trust in others is a popular virtue. The person who mistrusts other people is regarded as insecure, sick or both. Traditional wisdom has it that the only alternative to trust is distrust. Think about it for a moment. Trust involves expectation and obligation. When you trust someone, you expect them to behave in a certain way. If they fail to live up to your expectations, you feel they've let you down and sense that something has been lost from the relationship. If that someone is very close, the loss can be substantial. Suppose that you tell the other person how much you trust him or her to do such and such. You have obligated that person to behave as you want. Some parents do this with their children. They use trust to instill guilt. This pattern is repeated by the children when they grow up. The burden is passed on.

Trust in others weakens and pressures every relationship it touches. It imposes oughts and shoulds between you and me. I trust you to do what I know you *will* do, nothing more, nothing less. I hold no expectation and impose no obligation. In that way, we're both protected.

5. *Know your enemy and your friends.* Anyone who has competed in body contact sports knows the value of being able to stand in the opponent's shoes. Learning to think and move the way your enemy does gives you an edge. Miyamoto Musashi, the legendary sword fighter whom you met in the introduction to this book, urged the warrior to "become the enemy." Koichi Tohei, speaking much later, put it differently. He said that, in defending against an attack, you must "move when his (your opponent's) mind moves."

116

Knowing others involves much more than listening to their words and interpreting their body language. It means being open and receptive enough to sense their thoughts, think and feel as they do, and experience their happiness and—in some cases—their pain. Unless you really **know** the other person, you cannot help or even relate to them properly. And it's not always an easy task. It means that you must be free of judgment and able to observe calmly, clearly, and dispassionately. It means that you understand clearly the difference between responsibilities *to* and *for*. It is not a skill that is acquired easily.

It's probably easier to know a stranger than someone you love. Frequently, when you love someone, that love is conditional. You love what they are to you or what they can do for you. You unknowingly impose conditions of expectation and desire upon them with the result that the relationship becomes a negotiation. Subtly you bargain for what you want with what you are willing to give. Try though you may, if you love, you relinquish power and increase your own vulnerability. To love much is to accept the risk that you *may* be hurt. The only way out is to learn to love unconditionally, without expectation or demand. Unconditional love is powerful love. Unconditional love radiates outward like heat from a stove or ripples in a pool. It requires no object or incentive. It simply IS.

You want to know (become) others in order that you may respond appropriately, according to what IS rather than what appears to be. This awareness is both protective and healing in its effects. It protects you when others threaten and, depending on the strength of your love, heals them.

6. *Accept others as they are.* It's natural to want to share what you have, to show others the way. And it's often easy to see what others must do differently. "If only she would ———," the saying goes. The hard fact, however, is that where people are is where they should be at **that moment.** Your truth and mine are different, at least for now. I have things to learn and places to go before (and **if**) I'll be ready for your truth. We need to give each other room to grow.

This acceptance is critical in human relationships. It frees others from the weight of expectation and it encourages a mutual outflow of noncritical loving support. When I accept you as you are, I free myself to allow you to become what you can be.

7. *Act spontaneously.* I can't decide to be spontaneous any more than I can decide to be ten-feet tall. But I can provide the conditions that encourage spontaneity—stillness, listening, openness, curiosity, a sense of humor, a willingness to risk being wrong and to admit it when I am, and a sense that I'll be at the right place at the right time and have what I need. These are all aspects of the discovered self. My attentiveness to them ensures that I will recognize spontaneity when it knocks on my door. Spontaneity is response rather than reaction. If you push me and I resist, that's reaction. My reaction may be deliberate or the result of long conditioning, but it's not spontaneous. If you push and I yield—allow us to move effortlessly in the same direction and then adapt to your intent and redirect us both— that's response, and it can be spontaneous. Spontaneity frees me from the need to preplan or prejudge. It puts discovery into my life on a moment-by-moment basis.

8. *Recognize experience and crisis as learning.* If you accept purpose in your life, it's easier to understand that where you are now is appropriate and that what happens next will also be appropriate. When viewed in the context of a single life span, this may be hard to swallow. But when life is understood as transcending both birth and death, it makes sense. Seeing problems and crises as learning opportunities frees you to act rather than forcing you to react. In many instances the difference between a disaster and a blessing lies in this simple perspective. There is **always** a way out and up. The warrior strives constantly to get outside and above the problem.

9. *Know what you have to give.* I have something that is totally unique. You can't duplicate it or get it anywhere else. And so do you. We all have our own uniqueness that can never be taken away. The secret is to recognize what you have that's special, what you can do better than anyone else. When you discover that (and only you can discover it), you become powerful. You have center, balance, calm, and purpose all in one healthy being, and you can't be stopped. There are no exceptions. Every man, woman, and child has a unique identity. You don't create it, you become aware of it.

10. *Demand the best of yourself and others.* It's easier to

criticize poor performance than to demand excellence. It's also easy to make only negative demands. Remember in chapter 6 I said that you discover what your body **can** do rather than what it must be **made** to do? Demanding the best of yourself or of someone else is recognizing what you have to give. So many people fail in this recognition. They settle for less than they need to. We do this to ourselves and to others. We are sympathetic toward our friends' problems, tell them we know how bad they feel and how awful it must be. In so doing, we fail to meet our responsibilities TO. We fail to demand for them what we claim for ourselves. We bind rather than free. The demand that uplifts and heals is **always** positive. It is affirmation rather than denial.

11. *Realize purpose at work.* It's awfully easy to question events, bemoan our fate, and second-guess past performance. Self-flagellation has a kind of bittersweet attractiveness about it. We feel better because we've been able to beat on someone— ourselves. But self-criticism forces us to return to the arena of chance and the world of the constructed self.

We realize purpose when we become aware of a higher conformity and confident in the discovered self. Once we do, the pressure is off and we ascend upward.

12. *Extend positive power.* I can be negative more easily than I can be positive. It's fun to pick people apart, justify my mistakes, and point out how things could easily get worse. Negative power works that way. It feeds on my reaction and belief in order to bring me under its control.

Extending positive power requires constant, diligent effort. It's hard to believe you can fly when you've only crawled before, but you can. It just takes a little more time. And every soaring moment yields greater confidence. Positive power generates power.

Discovering More

Pursuit of the warrior strategies not only protects the discovered self, it leads to further discovery. In the next and last chapter are some discoveries of my own. They're pieces I've lifted, with some smoothing and editing, from a personal journal I've kept for more than ten years. They're about succeeding, competing, finishing things up, dying, and loving—topics most of us think about at one time or another. Try them as you would a new recipe, with an open mind and an adventurous spirit. They will tell you a bit more about where I've been. The last entry reports on where I **think** I am now, but doesn't attempt to predict where I'm going.

CHAPTER EIGHT
DISCOVERIES

If you have completed the work in chapter 3 you know that writing your autobiography can be a formidable task. Much less demanding, but equally rewarding, is the practice of keeping a personal journal of the kind I alluded to earlier. I'm not suggesting that you substitute journal writing for autobiography, but that you do both. Keeping a journal can do much for you. For one thing, it's a good way to monitor changes in your thinking. It also helps to improve your writing style.

I learned to write at the hands of a director I worked with many years ago in consulting. For more than two years, he smothered my writing efforts in corrective red ink. More than once I was ready to throw in the towel, but he convinced me it was worth the effort. One day he casually observed: "You know, I used to think that good writing was just another skill and that it didn't necessarily indicate how clearly a person thinks. But in watching consultants come and go, I've concluded that poor writing is a sign of sloppy thinking. Clear thinking and skilled writing are both a result of continuous writing and rewriting."

You don't have to be a good writer to keep a journal, but if you **do** keep one and write it in regularly, both your writing and your thinking will improve.

I like reading other people's journals. I guess I'm naturally nosey. Some authors write in a journal-like style. Hugh Prather writes that way. Reading his books gives me the feeling he's letting me in on his thinking. I often disagree with him I'm sure he expects that readers will, but it's fun comparing ideas. So I'm suggesting that, in addition to writing your own journal, it's useful to read what others have thought and written about topics that concern you.

The selections from my journal cover a wide range of subjects from learning to avoid failure to understanding what love is all about. These half dozen entries go back to the fall of 1972, but only the last one is dated. Each one was picked because it continues to live for me and represents an accurate statement of my current thinking. The last piece, "Return to the River," which was written in 1980, says as well as anything where I am now. It concludes gently and tentatively. And that's all right, because that's the way my life is today.

How Not to Fail

Kent is a whiz at math, something I've never been good at. He owns a company that does failure analysis, that is, advises clients how not to fail in their businesses. He doesn't tell them how to succeed, just how to avoid failing.

Chuck, a mutual friend, suggested that Kent and I get together. He said we had a lot in common. I'm always skeptical when someone tells me I ought to know a mathematician, but I agreed. Chuck managed to get us on a seminar program together as co-speakers. He was right. We do have a lot in common. We think about success and failure in much the same way.

Few people set out to fail. Most try to succeed and quite a few of them end up failing. Kent thinks that one reason is the logic difference between people who strive unabashedly for success and those who are alert to avoid failure. He talks about "or" and "and" gates—the mathematician's way of describing how we connect event and cause. He says that, to succeed at something, you have to do lots of things, all connected with "ands." In other words, there are certain conditions for success that must be present if you are to succeed. But, he says, it's much easier to fail. You have only to screw up on one of the "ors" and you're in trouble.

For example, assume I asked you what would be required to **successfully** go to the store and buy a pound of bacon. You would start by telling me that you would have to get your keys and money, and get in the car, and start the motor, and so on. If, on the other hand, I asked you what might cause you to fail in your mission, you might describe the same events and add others, but you would connect them with "ors" rather than "ands." Failure of any one of these "or" events could prevent you from succeeding. According to Kent, that's just what happens to many business people. They fail to bring home the bacon because they think only about becoming a smashing success and ignore events that might cause them to fail. It's not just a matter of the conjunctions they use. There are fundamental differences in attitude, and that's where Kent and I agree.

I've known high-powered entrepreneurs who looked only at the "ands" and ignored the "ors," and failed. They were so obsessed with making things happen that they impeded their own progress. They adopted single-minded goals and then tried to force-fit their lives to them. Their tactical genius tended to override their strategic good sense, because they never allowed themselves to gain a larger perspective. Conversely, I know others who have been spectacularly and effortlessly successful. They seem always to be listening for the "or," the still small voice that says, "no, not that way, **this** way." They are inner-directed and open-minded with respect to both their goals and the way they go about achieving them. And they differ from their more success-dominated colleagues in another respect; if they encounter a setback or fail, they seem to be uplifted by the experience. They see it (much like the eighth strategy discussed in the preceding chapter) as an opportunity to learn a needed lesson. They have a greater capacity to see more "ors." In other words, they're more aware of the things that impede and promote their growth.

Much of the current emphasis on short-range quantitative goals in individual and corporate planning is misplaced. It tends to force events rather than allowing them to happen. It discourages objective considerations of the "ors" and inhibits spontaneity. Once I commit myself to making something happen, come hell or high water, I've lost my objectivity. I may win battles here and there, but I'll lose in the long run. Kent is right. The people who think only of "ands" are different from the ones who think also about the "ors." Thanks, Chuck, for getting us together.

Beyond Competition

I guess I've fought two-hundred or more martial-arts contests. That's in addition to playing football, boxing, running track, and competing with just about everyone—including my wife and children—at one time or another. A while ago, I began to question the value of competition. When I started out, competing and winning were everything. Then, sometime after the canyon trip in 1972, I began to sense that the only worthwhile competition was the struggle with myself. Being a better person became better than beating someone else. Now I've begun to question the wisdom of even competing with myself. It seems to get in the way of allowing. I'm impressed by how much more easily things get done when I allow myself to excel. I discovered that I have more ability than I ever dreamed. Oh, I still like to better my running times in the 10K or come home knowing I've had a hard weight workout, but I'm more relaxed about it now. I think I'm better at listening these days. I hope so, because I'm working at it.

Completing the Past

It's odd how some people bottle things up. They feel that if they suppress and ignore what's bugging them, it will go away. I've noticed that seldom works. I've learned to sense when a person is being pushed around by the past.

A man enrolled in a self-defense class I taught. He was short and stocky, with graying hair and an uncertain manner. His eyes shifted uneasily and he moved awkwardly. He seemed almost apologetic about being in the class and was always the last to learn. I invited him to lunch one day. Amid the small talk that separates ordering and eating, he blurted out: "My father never taught me how to fight. He taught John, my older brother, but he never taught me. Why?"

An uncompleted past is like an infected wound. Sooner or later it boils up to the surface. I'm sure Dad's two strokes were caused by his bitterness over losing the farm. He **knew** it didn't help, but he wanted to get back at someone and prove he could still win.

Being angry or resentful and trying to settle old scores are examples of an uncompleted past. They reveal buried problems that are sure to erupt eventually. I can't afford to have things that haven't been dealt with lurking in my past. In all I've learned in the past twenty years, my sense tells me if it's foolish and dangerous to tolerate festering wounds. But how do you deal with something that you don't want to look at when it just won't go away?

There's a martial arts principle (*kime*) of focusing all of your attention and force on your opponent for the split second it takes to immobilize him or her and then instantly centering and being ready to refocus on the next attack. To get "stuck" on a single adversary is anathema to the martial artist. The martial artist practices long and hard to become fluid and flexible, to see things as they are, and to shift his focus quickly and easily. This tells me a lot about dealing with the past.

Getting stuck in a problem or being angry or resentful serves no useful purpose. It prevents me from seeing issues clearly, disposing of them quickly, and moving on to other things. I become captured by the problem or the situation. It's like trying **not** to think about something; that only ensures that it will remain there and fester.

You can't change past events, but you **can** alter your perception of them. We get trapped, not by the events themselves, but by our failure to understand their significance and blessed by them. So, how do you deal with something that's really tough, unpleasant, or frightening? Again, the analogy of the martial artist helps me. You deal with a situation by turning **your entire attention** to it—not your prejudice or your criticism— your attention. You see clearly and understand quickly, take appropriate action, and turn away without looking back. You are ruthless in refusing to be bugged by the past.

Looking back without judgment or criticism takes practice, especially if the wound is deep. It requires us to separate ourselves from our reactive patterns—guilt, fear, self-recrimination, and resentment. It means that we are truly willing to regard events as teachers. I'm convinced that, when we reach this stage, *we* determine the significance of events. We are the reason they have occurred and we survive their temporary reality. Then we're exhilarated and empowered by everything

127

that happens, confident in the present, and enthusiastic about the future.

The past is complete only when we're not bound to it or threatened by it, when we are at peace with it. And, sooner or later, we are moved to reach that state of peace.

Death Is a Narrow Place in the Rocks

BAJA, CALIFORNIA. It's June, 110 degrees in the sun. We are heading north on a Honda GL 1000 motorcycle, having spent ten days touring Baja. Time is short. We must make the ferry at Santa Rosalia by five o'clock for the trip across the Sea of Cortez to Mexico.

Traffic is light expect for an occasional truck, a large semi, and another cycle heading south. We are cruising at fifty to seventy, opening up on the straightaway and drawing down on the curves. The heat, narrow roads, and tight deadline combine to produce an uncomfortable feeling of pressure. The trip has been good till this point. Now things don't seem quite right. They don't fit together as they should. Later, we will both confess to having been apprehensive about the morning's start.

We come out of a turn into a long straight stretch, then an S curve, first to the right then climbing back to the left. Suddenly in the second turn and without warning, the bike is down, sliding in a shower of sparks toward an open ditch. One-inch crashbars are ground in half, mirrors and windshield torn away, and the cycle flips.

I am lying partly under the bike. Carol is somewhere else. I struggle to separate myself from the wreck, wrists painfully sprained and, as I discover later, my left arm a mass of cuts, bruises, and blood. Carol is all right, only minor scrapes. We're both alive. We see the cause of the spill, a long, ugly black swath of gas and oil extending to a service station 200 yards to the north.

We manage to clean up enough to drive to a public medical center about thirteen kilometers up the road. The bike is rideable. The windshield broke neatly so that, at ten yards away, it gives the bike a low rakish look. Only as you get closer and see the scrapes, blood, and torn jeans do you realize that all is not right.

We go on because there is nothing else to do. The border, McDonalds, and a soft bed are still two days away. We will make it one way or another. We cross the last hundred miles of the Sonora desert the next day, Carol feeding me ice cubes from a dripping bag set between us to keep me conscious under the burning heat, now 115 degrees.

Crashing a cycle, if you live, is a good learning experience. You analyze, wonder, and speculate, Was it my fault? What really caused it? How could it have been avoided? What should we do differently the next time, if there is one? Answers to these questions came slowly over the next few weeks. But they were not the important answers, or even the important questions.

Many who have walked the narrow line between life and death report a certain calmness, a kind of supreme objectivity, as though in the middle of the terror there is peace. They often say that in those critical moments, they don't think about themselves or about their own safety. My first thoughts were: "We're going down. Is Carol all right? Will the bike make it to the border?" No thoughts of me, of survival, or of death.

In the weeks that followed, I puzzled about my reactions. It was gratifying to know that self-concern and fear were not uppermost in my mind. It was as though I'd welcomed the challenge once its inevitability became apparent. But what of death, the end of it all? Why had **that** not been important?

My mind kept turning it over, thoughts returning to an earlier scene, a hazy memory. I was walking in a canyon, high walls of reddish rock on either side. Ahead the path grew narrower and the terrain steeper. The canyon seemed to stop, close out. As I got nearer, I saw there was a narrow slot in the rocks only a little wider than my shoulders. I hastened the climb, increasing effort if not pace, eager to know what was on the other side.

As I squeezed through the opening and saw the widening valley beyond, I stopped. There, on the ground in front of me scarcely a yard ahead, was the decayed carcus of a jackrabbit, bones white in the sun.

It made it through the tight squeeze and into the sun and the valley beyond. And when it did, it no longer needed the old body it had been dragging along. It left it along with other artifacts of its past, and went on.

Death is a narrow place in the rocks. I've seen it close at hand more than once and am unimpressed by its threat or its promise. It is but one more passage in life's longer journey. Its power over us stems from its boasts of finality and mystery. But when we approach the crevice and stand in the shadow, we can see the light beyond. We know that all we lose is our burden, the accumulated weight of our beliefs and fears that are no longer necessary or real.

Death offers nothing and gives less. It is a momentary pause on the path that enables us to see a bit more clearly. It has only the power we give it, the mystery we grant. It is nature's last and greatest joke on us, a cause for laughter rather than crying, for when it's over, we know we've won.

Love Is Power

Power isn't muscle, money, position, or prestige; it's love. The apparently accidental lessons I've been forced to learn about love aren't accidental at all; they're the gentle prodding of His rod and His staff. Why has it taken me so long to see this?

Learning just how powerful love *is* takes time. As children, we need, want, and depend more than we love. As adults we use love as a weapon and barter to get what we want. When we marry, especially if we marry young, we're often better at sex than love, and constantly confuse the two. If we're experienced, we use sex as a crutch or a club. If we're not, we fear it and worry that too much or too little will spoil everything. We're caught leaning on each other and denying our own inexperience.

I guess it's natural to regard love in terms of a single person or relationship. When we do, we reveal our humanness and our vulnerability, for seldom is love for another free of expectation or demand. If I love you exclusively and totally, I give you the power to hurt me when you fail to meet my expectations. In daring to love we attest our willingness to learn more about the true nature of love, a love of acceptance in which openness and honesty rather than defensiveness and deceit prevail. We open ourselves to sometimes hard lessons but, in so doing, demonstrate our confidence in a higher, more all-encompassing love.

Sometimes, if we're very fortunate, we meet someone with a special kind of love and patience who comes into our life by design, but who appears with the beauty of coincidence, someone who comes to learn and stays to teach.

When this happens, we grow. We approach a new and deeper sense of love where words like selfishness, sin, and hate are irrelevant. We learn that happiness is finding joy in and where we are, NOW. For a while at least, we cease wanting and striving and begin to live.

Love is the sum of all we discover about ourselves. It is stillness, exhilaration, openness, and laughter. It is conforming to a higher authority. It is the only thing that really grows with giving. We become stronger, warmer, and able to give more, see further, and fly higher. Love is the ultimate power, to be reflected and shared but never possessed.

No sharing can be total. No matter how much we give, there is more to be given. No matter how much we learn, there is more to be learned. No matter how closely two lives are entwined, there is still more to love. Love is infinite, limitless.

> Love is not lost in giving, only in taking.
> Love begins with oneself and radiates outward.
>
> Love that begins in weakness becomes a demand.
> Love that begins in strength is a gift.
>
> Love and freedom are joined. True love liberates.
> Imperfect love binds, holds, and owns.
>
> Love is the recognition of our essential oneness.
> We need only to see it.

We discover love within ourselves and share it with others. It is important that we take time for the discovery and dedicate ourselves to the sharing. In my life, I have had the unspeakable joy of sharing. This is what it means to me.

• Let us live as much as possible so that in each moment of every day, our lives are ennobled, strengthened, and directed by this inner fire, this silent purpose.

• Let not bitterness govern our least thought or action, but rather, let the cancer of bitterness be dissolved with the power of love, pure, undemanding, and constant.

• Only in the quiet stillness of our inner thoughts can we perceive the love that has brought and bound us together.

• Never, even for an instant, no matter where you are or what you're doing, are you beyond the touch of my love. When you least expect it, you will see its sign—in a warm breeze, a yellow daisy, or a soft starry night. It will touch you, caress you, hold you. But do not reach for it and grasp it, or you may crush it.

• The intense love, joy, and enthusiasm for life that I share with you is my testimony of gratitude for all that God has done for me.

• There is no night so dark that it is not followed by day, no storm so violent that it is not ended by calm, no hate so virulent that it cannot be replaced by love.

• Though the years of our passage are few, they are sufficient to aid us in our discoveries of the limitless nature of our true being.

• Our lives are a rite of purification in which the fragile branches of the past, strengthened and enlarged by the continued alternation of sun and wind, grow into the supporting and sheltering limbs of the future.

• Space and time are limits to be overcome as we progress from being lonely, to being alone, to being together.

• Not one leaf falls without His knowing. You are as precious to Him as you are to me and I to you. Just as you cannot stray from the reach of my love, so you can never for a moment be outside of His care. His love and mine surround you, guard you, guide you, and His love is so great that the immense love I have for you is still the smallest part.

• Love makes whole and heals. The secret of healing *is* love, not a love of needing or wanting, but of having and giving. Healing love requires no object and knows no limit. It is unceasing in effect, incontestable in its power, and all inclusive in its presence.

Return to the River

> The Potomac River
> Great Falls, Virginia
> October, 1980

It's more than eight years since I began the trip down the Green River. I left the Grand Canyon and came here to the Potomac.

Sitting here, high on a rock wall above the river, I realize that water is important in my life. It is my peace, my meditation, the gentle prod that moves me from the world of minute details and constant problems to broad outlines and developing possibilities. Why? Why the canyon, the Potomac, or the Bay off Cape Cod where I've spent countless hours these past years?

The river gathers sticks and sand as it moves. I grasp meaning in the same way, in bits and pieces. The ocean works it's ceaseless rhythm and gradually alters the shoreline. Its dependability and gentle lulling sounds mask its tremendous force. I am comfortable working in the same way, chewing away at things and, like the ebbing outward tide, withdrawing for a while, only to come back later with renewed force.

Mine is not the structured learning of the classroom or the faith-filled acceptance of the church. It is the gradual discovery of my inner being and my place in a larger order. I learn through experience, my own. I find that my experience works *for* me to the degree that I do not fear life, require public approval, or avoid private censure, which are self-limits. I've learned that the price of growth is being willing to go it alone, to listen to the inner voice when others are screaming and arguing otherwise. No matter how skilled, how loving, how willing are the words and acts of another, the choice and path are mine. When I listen for the inner voice, it speaks to me, tells me when I'm on the right course, and lets me discover for myself.

Here at this moment, beside the river, there is no time. All is intact, neatly held within the present world of experience. Past and future are smoothly blended in the present mingling of earth and sky and water. What is, is made up of what was, and what may be is unimportant until it becomes *now*. The rocks, rapids, and still waters are part of my now, part of me.

I am of the land. I find that certain places represent a universal belonging, a joining to the earth that strengthens and grounds. This rooting is both physical and spiritual. It begins with the solid outlines of trees and rocks and expands into the subtle hues of reflected sky and gently moving water, until a sense of oneness and belonging surrounds me. I am at peace, at home in this world.

My path and my world are magical voyages of discovery. Yet nothing is truly seen until it is shared. Sharing is both the price and the reward of being fully alive. Until I give of that which I have discovered, it is not mine. And so I give, with love.

AUTHOR'S NOTE

One of the rewards of writing and speaking is the ensuing dialogue that inevitably occurs between the author/speaker and his audience. If you have been stimulated by this book and perhaps sense the emergence of the warrior spirit within yourself, and would like to share your thoughts, I would love to hear from you. Drop me a line care of The Delta Group, Inc. 1523 Mo

245 Ponderosa Way
Evergreen, CO 80439
303/674-9850

Shale Paul

BIBLIOGRAPHY

The books listed below have been grouped into eight categories for your convenience. Where a book fits into more than one category, a comment to that effect follows the entry. I have also taken the liberty of commenting on some entries.

Consciousness Research

Cade, C. Maxwell, and Coxhead, Nona. *The Awakened Mind: Biofeedback and the Development of Higher States of Awarenss.* New York: Dell Publishing Company, 1980.

Ornstein, Robert E., ed. *The Nature of Human Consciousness: A Book of Readings.* San Francisco: W. H. Freeman and Company, 1973.

———. *The Psychology of Consciousness.* New York: Pelican Books, 1979.

Tart, Charles T., ed. *Altered States of Consciousness.* New York: Doubleday and Company, 1972.

Martial Arts

General Readings

Draeger, Donn F., and Smith, Robert W. *Comprehensive Asian Fighting Arts.* Tokyo, Japan: Kodansha International. Offers a panoramic view of fighting arts in eleven Asian Countries.

Harrison, E. J. *The Fighting Spirit of Japan: The Esoteric Study of the Martial Arts and Way of Life in Japan.* London and New York: W. Foulsham & Co. Ltd., undated. This is one of the earliest English-language texts on the esoteric aspects of the martial arts. Harrison, a writer for several Japanese newspapers and for the *London Daily Mail* around 1900 was an avid Judo enthusiast. His work still ranks as a monument in the field.

Ratti, Oscar, and Westbrook, Adele. *Secrets of the Samurai: A Survey of the Martial Arts of Feudal Japan* Rutland, Vermont, and Tokyo, Japan: Charles E. Tuttle Company, 1973. An excellent overview of the history and culture of Japanese martial arts. Part III, "Inner Factors of Bujutsu," presents an in-depth discussion of the concepts of the center (*hara*) and power (*ki*), and some of the strategies underlying the martial arts.

Aikido and Ki-Aikido

Ratti, Oscar and Westbrook, Adele. *Aikido and the Dynamic Sphere: An Illustrated Introduction.* Rutland, Vermont, and Tokyo, Japan: Charles E. Tuttle Company, 1974. A thorough and scholarly presentation of the art of aikido, including history, theory, and practice.

Tohei, Koichi. *This Is Aikido: With Mind and Body Co-ordinated.* San Francisco, Calif. and Tokyo, Japan: Japan Publications, Inc., 1975. This is a text on ki-aikido techniques as taught by the master, Koichi Tohei. Dr. Tohei studied Zen under master Josei Ohta of the Daitokuji temple in Kyoto, misogi breathing from master Tetsuji Ogura, and aikido from master and founder, Morihei Ueshiba. Dr. Tohei founded Shinshin Toitsu Aikido (Aikido with Mind and Body Coordinated) in 1974 and is currently president of the Ki Society International.

————. *Ki in Daily Life.* Elmsford, N.Y., San Francisco, Calif. and Tokyo, Japan: Ki No Kenkyukai H.Q., 1978. Presents principles and applications of ki training, based on Dr. Tohei's ki-aikido system.

Judo

Dainippon Yubenkai Kodansha. *Illustrated Kodokan Judo.* Tokyo, Japan: Dianippon Printing Company, Ltd., 1955. An early text that has been superseded by many others, yet that nonetheless epitomizes judo form and technique.

Mifune, Kyuzo. *Canon of Judo.* Tokyo, Japan: Seibundo-Shinkosa Publishing Company, 1956. Mr. Mifune, who passed on at the age of eighty-four, is a legend in judo. During my stay in Japan (1957–58), he was still practicing actively and continued to maintain his competitive weight of approximately 110 pounds.

Watanabe, Jiichi, and Avakian, Lindy. *The Secrets of Judo.* Rutland, Vermont, and Tokyo, Japan: Charles E. Tuttle Company, 1960. Despite its rather unfortunate title, this text presents a clear explanation of judo techniques.

Karate

Nishiyama, Hidetaka, and Brown, Richard C. *Karate: The Art of Empty Hand Fighting.* Rutland, Vermont, and Tokyo, Japan: Charles E. Tuttle Company, 1960. Bookshelves have been flooded with karate books since this book was published, but it is still a good text, particulary for the reader who wants an overall view.

Zen

Herrigel, Eugen. *The Method of Zen.* New York: Vintage Books, 1974.

———. *Zen in the Art of Archery.* New York: Vintage Books, 1971.

Kapleau, Philip, ed. and comp. *Three Pillars of Zen: Teaching, Practice, Enlightenment.* Boston: Beacon Press, 1965.

Legget, Trevor, comp. and trans. *A First Zen Reader.* Rutland, Vermont, and Tokyo, Japan: Charles E. Tuttle Company, 1960.

Miura, Isshu, and Sasaki, Ruth Fuller. *The Zen Koan.* New York: Harcourt, Brace, & World, Inc., 1965.

Ross, Nancy Wilson, ed. *The World of Zen: An East-West Anthology.* New York: Vintage Books, 1960.

Sekida, Katsuki. *Zen Training: Methods and Philosophy.* New York and Tokyo: John Weatherhill, Inc., 1975.

Suzuki, Daisetz T. *Zen and Japanese Culture.* Bollingen Series. New York: Pantheon Books, Inc., 1959. In contrast to the more method-oriented books above, Suzuki offers a panoramic view of Zen and its effects on many aspects of Japanese culture.

Watts, Alan W. *The Way of Zen.* New York: Vintage Books, 1957. Watts, a westerner, has written many books on

Zen. This one is a good introductory text and, in many respects, is better than some of his later ones.

Meditation, Western Style

Carrington, Patricia. *Freedom in Meditation.* New York: Anchor books, 1978. If you like meditation stripped of all its esoteric trappings, this book should do it. Dr. Carrington has developed a method that she calls "Clinically Standardized Meditation." Her book is a good background for the new student who wants to learn generally what meditation is all about.

Gendlin, Eugene T. *Focusing.* New York: Everest House, 1978. "Focusing" is the term given by Gendlin to his problem-solving technique. While the technique is not termed meditation, it makes use of altered states as a basis on which the problem-solving actions take place.

Hendricks, Gay, and Wills, Russel. *The Centering Book: Awareness Activities for Children, Parents, and Teachers* Englewood Cliffs, N.J.: Prentice-Hall, 1975. Actually, there are now three centering books in this series. They contain useful exercises for teachers, parents, anyone interested in teaching simple centering techniques.

LeShan, Lawrence, *How to Meditate: A Guide to Self-Discovery.* New York: Bantam Books, 1974. LeShan's system for categorizing the many forms of meditation is a bit complicated, but the book as a whole is concise and pragmatic.

Christian Science

Eddy, Mary Baker. *Science and Health with Key to the Scriptures.* Boston: Published under the Will of Mary Baker Eddy, 1875 (original copyright). This is the textbook of Christian Science, written by Mrs. Eddy over a hundred years ago and revised successively until her death in 1910. I have included it, as well as the biographical references below, because Christian Science and Mrs. Eddy have unquestionably had an early and significant effect on my life.

Peel, Robert. *Mary Baker Eddy: The Years of Discovery.* New York, Chicago, San Francisco: Holt, Rinehart and Winston, 1966.

————. *Mary Baker Eddy: The Years of Trial.* New York, Chicago, San Francisco: Holt, Rinehart and Winston, 1971.

————. *Mary Baker Eddy: The Years of Authority.* New York: Holt, Rinehart and Winston, 1977.

Strategy

Castaneda, Carlos. *The Teachings of Don Juan: A Yaqui Way of Knowledge.* New York: Pocket Books, 1976.

————. *A Separate Reality: Further Conversations with Don Juan.* New York: Pocket Books, 1976.

————. *Journey to Istlan: The Lessons of Don Juan.* New York: Pocket Books, 1976.

————. *Tales of Power.* New York: Pocket Books, 1976.

These four books should be read in sequence. Readers may quarrel with their categorization as "strategy," for they are much more.

Mushashi, Miyamoto. *A Book of Five Rings: A Guide to Strategy* by Victor Harris, copyright © 1974. Woodstock, N.Y.: Overlook Press, 1974.

Fitness, Sports, and Nutrition

Anderson, Bob. *Stretching.* Bolinas, Calif.: Shelter Publications, 1981.

Bailey, Covert. *Fit or Fat: A New Way to Health and Fitness through Nutrition and Aerobic Exercise.* Boston: Houghton Mifflin Company, 1978.

Cooper, Kenneth, H., M.D. *The Aerobics Way.* New York: Bantam Books, 1978.

Cooper, Mildred and Kenneth H. *Aerobics for Women.* New York: Bantam Books, 1979.

Nutrition Search, Inc. *Nutrition Almanac.* New York: McGraw-Hill Book Company, 1979.

Sheehan, George. *This Running Life.* New York: Simon and Schuster, 1980.

Murphy, Michael, and White, Rhea A. *The Psychic Side of Sports.* Reading, Mass.: Addison-Wesley Publishing Company, 1978.

BIBLIOGRAPHY

McCluggage, Denise. *The Centered Skier.* New York: Warner Books, 1977.

Nideffer, Robert M. *The Inner Athlete: Mind Plus Muscle for Winning.* New York: Thomas Y. Crowell, Publishers, 1976.

General Reading

Boyd, Doug. *Rolling Thunder.* New York: Dell Publishing Company, 1980.

Capra, Fritjof. *The Tao of Physics.* New York: Bantam Books, 1977.

Crystal, John C., and Bolles, Richard N. *Where Do I Go From Here With My Life?* Berkeley, Calif.: Ten Speed Press, 1974.

Ferguson, Marilyn. *The Aquarian Conspiracy: Personal Transformation in the 1980s.* Los Angeles, Calif. J.P. Tarcher, Inc., 1980. For those of you who doubt that anything is happening out there, Marilyn Ferguson's book provides a wealth of evidence that people are changing, everywhere!

Monroe, Robert A. *Journeys Out of the Body.* New York: Doubleday Press, 1973. This book is somewhat dated, simply because Mr. Monroe's research has progressed so much further in the past ten years. It does, however, give you some idea of what it's like in the out-of-body state.

Prather, Hugh. *Notes on Love and Courage.* New York: Doubleday and Company, Inc., 1977. Hugh Prather has written several books, including *Notes to Myself: I Touch the Earth, The Earth Touches Me* and *There Is a Place Where You Are Not Alone.*

Sheehy, Gail. *Pathfinders: Overcoming the Crises of Adult Life and Finding Your Own Path to Well-Being.* New York: William Morrow and Company, Inc., 1981. This is a sequel to Gail Sheehy's earlier work, *Passages.* It looks at people who have successfully negotiated some of the crises that confront us all.